Mathilda Masters

Illustrations by Louize Perdieus

123
SERIOUSLY
SMART THINGS
YOU NEED TO KNOW ABOUT THE
CLIMATE

123
SERIOUSLY SMART THINGS
YOU NEED TO KNOW
ABOUT THE CLIMATE

CONTENTS

FOREWORD

It's great that you're reading this book, because it's about some really important subjects: the climate and the environment.

The climate is changing. Of course, it's always changing, but now these changes are happening much faster than ever, which is a problem. The earth's average temperature is rising and human beings are to blame. The heating of the earth has serious consequences. The ice at the poles is melting, there are more storms and we need to think carefully about how we are going to grow enough food to feed everyone in the future.

Our environment is suffering. Forests are disappearing and many animals and plants are dying out. In the meantime, we're producing so much rubbish that we can't even get rid of it any more. There's even plastic in the deepest part of the ocean.

Luckily, more and more smart people are looking for solutions to these problems. Unfortunately, some people still claim that the situation isn't really that bad. If you want to prove them wrong, then you'll find plenty of information in this book to help you.

I put together this collection of 123 seriously smart facts with Hans Bruyninckx. Hans is director of the European Environment Agency, where they know a lot about the environment and climate. Science journalist Ilja Van Braeckel read the book to make sure there were no mistakes, and Louize Perdieus did the illustrations.

I hope you enjoy your journey of discovery. And don't forget to switch the lights off when you've finished reading!

Mathilda Masters

1

EVERYTHING IS CONNECTED

1 EVERYWHERE HAS A CLIMATE, WHATEVER THE WEATHER

The **climate** is the typical weather that occurs in a particular place on the earth. Scientists describe it as the average measurements of temperature, wind, humidity, snow and rain in a specific region over a period of about 30 years. Climate involves a variety of factors that work together. As you know, the earth revolves around the sun. The sun's rays hit the band around the middle of the earth, called the equator, more directly than the North and South Poles. So the sun's rays are more concentrated at the equator.

That means the climate is hot and tropical on the equator and cold at the North and South Poles. In between these extremes is an area with a temperate climate, generally not as hot as on the equator but less cold than in the polar regions.

Winds and ocean currents depend on the sun. This is because heat from the sun moves the air and water. Wind is air in motion. As hot air rises it collides with cold air, and wind is produced.

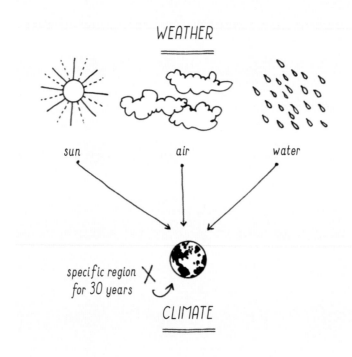

WEATHER

sun   air   water

specific region for 30 years

CLIMATE

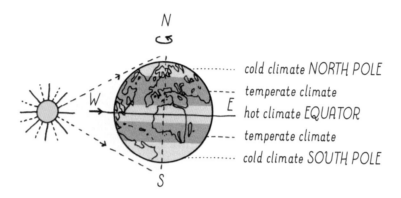

cold climate *NORTH POLE*
temperate climate
hot climate *EQUATOR*
temperate climate
cold climate *SOUTH POLE*

Ocean currents are also caused by temperature differences. These are called **convection currents**. The wind and the ocean currents work a bit like an enormous conveyor belt. They shift heat from one part of the earth to another.

We can't do very much to change our weather. Which is just as well, because otherwise you might arrange things so that it was sunny every day and it hardly ever rained. After a while, we would be living in a desert.

So we can't choose the weather, but that doesn't mean that people have no influence over the climate. You can read more about that later on in this book.

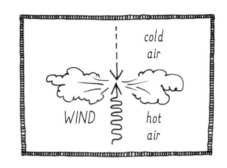

cold air

WIND   hot air

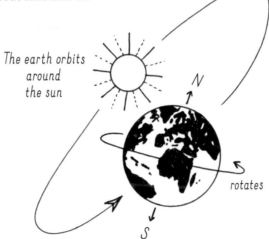

The earth orbits around the sun

N

rotates

S

2 PREDICTING THE WEATHER

Have you ever wondered just how weather forecasters predict the weather? They use a variety of tools, some of which were invented hundreds of years ago.

- A **hygrometer** measures humidity – this is the amount of water vapour that's in the air. In 1452, the Italians invented a kind of hygrometer, made from a pair of scales with a sponge hanging down. A wet sponge weighs more than a dry one, so you could measure the humidity from the weight.

- In the 16th century, the scientist Galileo Galilei invented a type of **thermometer**. It was made of glass balls filled with coloured liquid, which floated inside a closed tube filled with water. You could more or less tell how hot

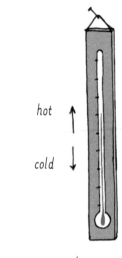

hot ↑

cold ↓

thermometer

it was from the height of the balls. Then, in the 17th century, someone called Gabriel Fahrenheit (sounds familiar doesn't it?) came up with the idea of using mercury to make the measurement more accurate. The mercury thermometer is still used today.

- In the 17th century, some people kept little weather houses. A weather house had two doors. Behind one was a model of a man holding an umbrella and behind the other was a woman with a parasol. The figures stood on a bar, hanging from a piece of dried sheep's gut. When the weather was dry, the sheep's gut got shorter and the little woman came out. When it was wet, the sheep's gut got longer and the man came out with his umbrella. Not a very accurate device!

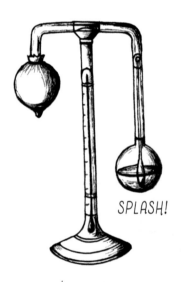

SPLASH!

hygrometer

A CUCKOO IDEA!

weather house

- The weight of the air pushes down on the earth. This is called air pressure, and it can be measured with an instrument called a **barometer**. When air pressure changes quickly, the weather changes too. As the air pressure rises, it usually means that fine weather is coming. If the air pressure drops, it's time to grab your umbrella!

the **Beaufort scale**. The Beaufort scale goes from 0 to 12, with 0 meaning calm or no wind and up to force 12 which is a hurricane. When the wind reaches force 8, you'd better brace yourself. That's a strong gale, gusting at 62 to 74 kilometres an hour. Hold on to your hat!

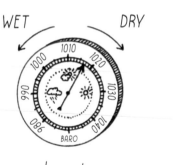

WET   DRY

barometer

- Wind speed is measured with an **anemometer**, a small windmill mounted on a tall shaft. It is made up of three or four hollow cups. The faster the mill spins, the harder the wind is blowing. Wind speed is also measured using

WHOOSH!

anemometer

17 to 35 km

* IT'S HOT AND HUMID UP HERE

weather balloon with a radiosonde

3 UP, UP AND AWAY

Have you ever seen a white balloon high up in the sky with a small parcel hanging under it? It was probably a **weather balloon** and the parcel is a machine called a **radiosonde**. Weather stations launch weather balloons twice a day. They are filled with a gas called helium and climb to a height of 17 to 35 kilometres. The higher the balloons go, the bigger they become, because the air becomes thinner and thinner and air pressure drops. As the pressure on the outside falls, the balloon grows larger. An average flight lasts two hours. The radiosonde measures temperature, humidity and air pressure. All the information is then sent back to weather stations. There are nearly ten thousand of these worldwide. Weather forecasters can predict the weather from the information the balloons send back. Special weather balloons called **ozonesondes** measure the amount of ozone in the air. Fact 8 will tell you a lot more about ozone. If you find a weather balloon in your garden, you can keep it or dispose of it as household waste. Some radiosondes have an address written on them, so you could always post them back to where they came from.

4 CLIMATE AND ENVIRONMENT ARE ALWAYS CONNECTED

The **environment** is our surroundings, the air we breathe, the water and the earth. The **natural environment** is made up of all living and non-living things that are not made by people – rocks, water and sand, as well as plants and animals. All these things are connected and they need each other. Humans and a lot of other animals need clean air to breathe. Plants make oxygen but, in turn, they mostly need clean water and nutritious soil. The climate is also an important part of the environment.

The climate and the environment are closely linked. Plants and animals are found in a particular climate. For instance, the very dry hot climate of the desert is ideal for camels and cactuses. You find elk and wolves in a colder climate where there are large forests. Penguins and seals like ice-cold water. You mostly see butterflies and bees in warm places where there are a lot of flowering plants. We call this kind of interdependence an **ecosystem**. Ecosystems have existed on the earth for millions of years and they usually change very slowly.

Sadly, humans can cause damage to ecosystems. We disturb the balance by cutting down forests, polluting the water and the air, and also causing climate change. As a result, many animal species have become rarer or are even extinct. Some suffocate in the plastic waste that people leave behind everywhere while others no longer have food because the seas are so polluted and overfished. What is bad for the environment is also bad for humans, because we are a part of the environment too.

HAND IN HAND
WITH PLANTS
ALL OVER THE COUNTRY

ecosystem

5 THE SUN GIVES OUT TEN THOUSAND TIMES MORE ENERGY THAN WE NEED

Chances are, you've never really given the sun that much thought, apart from feeling happy when it's warm and sunny. The sun is basically an enormous power station. It gives off, or emits, as much as 8,700 times more energy to the earth than we need for the whole world to keep everything working. However, not all of the sun's rays reach the earth's surface. About a third are immediately reflected back into space by clouds in the air, snow, ice and water on the earth's surface and other reflective surfaces. This reflection is called **albedo** (see Fact 32).

Two-thirds of all the sun's rays are absorbed by the earth and its atmosphere. The earth re-releases some of the energy as **infrared rays** and this creates heat. Yes, you read that right: the sun warms the earth and the earth warms the air. Some of the heat given off by the earth disappears into space, but some of it is bounced back again by gases in our atmosphere (see Fact 6). The balance between the sun's radiation and the earth's radiation is called the **global radiation balance**. It's very important that this balance is maintained.

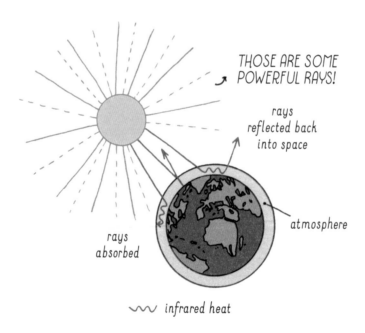

THOSE ARE SOME POWERFUL RAYS!

rays reflected back into space

atmosphere

rays absorbed

∿ infrared heat

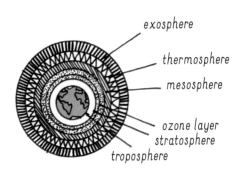

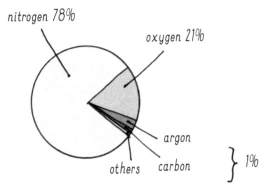

nitrogen 78%

oxygen 21%

exosphere

thermosphere

mesosphere

ozone layer
stratosphere

troposphere

argon

others   carbon

} 1%

6 THE EARTH IS AN ENORMOUS GREENHOUSE

You've probably seen **greenhouses** before. They're big glass buildings in which all kinds of delicious vegetables, fruits and other plants are grown. The sun shines in through the glass and this makes everything nice and warm. Heat is trapped inside, so plants keep growing even if it's cold outside.

Think of our planet as a giant greenhouse. Although it doesn't have glass around it, it does have a lot of gases. These gases make up the earth's **atmosphere**. Most of the atmosphere is made up of the gases nitrogen (78%) and oxygen (21%). The rest (1%) is mostly argon, but there are also greenhouse gases like methane and nitrous oxide. Around 2 to 3% of the atmosphere is water vapour, which is also a greenhouse gas. Greenhouse gases work like the glass of a greenhouse. In the daytime, the sun warms the outside of our planet. When the earth cools down at night, the greenhouse gases keep in the heat. They are like the roof and walls of our planet's greenhouse. Because of them, it is nice and warm in many places on the earth and lots of things can grow and bloom there. Without greenhouse gases,

it would be a lot colder on earth – an average of -18°C instead of the average global temperature of 15°C that we have now. That's a difference of as much as 33°C. It's likely that life on our planet would look very different!

So we need **greenhouse gases** to survive. But here's the problem. If there are too many greenhouse gases in the atmosphere, the earth keeps getting warmer. That's not a good thing and the consequences are dangerous. The ice at the poles melts and more water flows into the oceans. Large areas of land will flood. In some places, it will be so dry that nothing can grow any more, while other places overflow. There will also be more storms and hurricanes. These effects are called **climate change**.

7 YOU ARE A CARBON DIOXIDE FACTORY

Breathe in. Your lungs fill with oxygen. Breathe out again. A cloud of **carbon dioxide** comes out of your mouth. Don't worry, this is quite normal. Every creature that breathes in oxygen or O_2 produces carbon dioxide or CO_2. Plants convert it back into oxygen using photosynthesis (see Fact 9).

BREATHE IN BREATHE OUT

But it's not just humans and animals that create carbon. Most CO_2 is made by burning **fossil fuels**: oil, natural gas and coal. These were made when plants and animals that died millions of years ago were squashed together deep underground. Humans discovered that burning them created lots of energy. The uses of fossil fuels include powering machinery, heating houses, driving cars and running factories, to name but a few. Unfortunately, burning them releases a lot of CO_2.

This stays in the atmosphere and makes the earth warmer. You can't feel, touch, smell or see CO_2, but it's there.

Other natural **greenhouse gases** that are in the atmosphere are water vapour, methane, nitrous oxide and ozone. Water vapour is produced as water evaporates in the heat of the sun. It carries heat from the warm parts to the colder parts of the earth. Methane comes mainly from grazing animals, such as cows, and it's one of the causes of global warming. Nitrous oxide is a very powerful greenhouse gas that comes from soil that has been spread with fertilizer. Ozone is a greenhouse gas that is both positive and negative. It protects the planet against the harmful ultraviolet rays of the sun (see Fact 8). Without the ozone layer, it would be much harder to live on our planet. But it can also be a bad thing if it gets too close to the earth (see Fact 56). Then, it can affect our lungs and stop plants growing properly.

8 WATCH OUT FOR HOLES!

So you've been at the beach all day but you forgot to put on your sunscreen. When you get home, you're the same colour as a lobster. Ow, it hurts! Blame it on the ultraviolet rays of the sun. It's all down to them.

Luckily, there's a gas that protects us from most ultraviolet rays. It's called **ozone**. The ozone layer is in the **stratosphere**, about 20 kilometres above the earth at the tropics, around 12 kilometres in the temperate zones, and even lower at the poles. The ozone layer is very important. If it wasn't there, we wouldn't be able to live on earth.

In the 1970s, scientists discovered a problem with the ozone layer. It was getting thinner and thinner and holes were appearing in it, especially above the South Pole. This effect was caused by chemicals called **chlorofluorocarbons**, also known as **CFCs** or propellants. These were used in aerosol cans and in fridges and freezers, among other

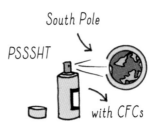

South Pole

PSSSHT

with CFCs

hole in the ozone layer

things. When CFCs came into contact with an ozone molecule, they broke down one of its three oxygen molecules. This left only O_2 or oxygen, letting the ultraviolet rays through. Luckily, a lot of countries signed a treaty banning CFCs. It was quite a long time before the hole began to mend itself. In 2000 it was at its largest, the same size as the whole of North America. But by 2017, satellite photographs showed that the hole had grown smaller again. Scientists are keeping a very close watch on the ozone layer. Climate change could create more holes, but the ozone layer might also grow so thick that not enough ultraviolet light would get through. A hole isn't a good thing, but then too much ozone would be bad thing too!

SUNSHINE!   OUCH!

There's a hole in the ozone layer!

9 PLANTS HELP US TO BREATHE

If you could travel back in time billions of years, you'd find the earth was a very different place. Not only were there no animals or people, but the earth's atmosphere was mainly made up of carbon dioxide and there was no oxygen. Then, tiny plants called algae started growing in the oceans. They fed on the carbon dioxide and at the same time they made oxygen.

Then, millions of years later, living creatures that breathed oxygen evolved. This was how the **carbon cycle** developed. The leaves and needles of plants and trees, most algae and some bacteria took carbon dioxide or CO_2 from the air. With water and sunlight, CO_2 is converted into sugars that plants can feed on. The process is called **photosynthesis**. At the same time, all these plants, algae and bacteria produce oxygen, which humans and other animals need to survive. So as you can see, everything on our planet is interconnected. All living things depend on each other.

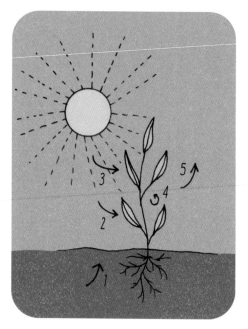

photosynthesis

1. plant takes water from the soil

2. leaves take carbon dioxide from the air

3. plant gets energy from sunlight through its leaves

4. plant turns water and carbon dioxide into sugars and oxygen

5. plant lets out oxygen into the air and uses sugars to grow

This means that woods and rainforests are hugely important to life on earth, and so are the lakes and seas where algae grow. Did you know that a large 100-year-old oak tree can make enough oxygen for ten people to breathe?

All around the world, from the forests of Russia, Europe and North America to the rainforests in the tropics, trees absorb a lot of carbon dioxide. The trees in the northern taiga are mostly coniferous. That means they keep their needles all year round, so they absorb CO_2 constantly.

Woodlands with mainly deciduous trees (they lose their leaves in the autumn) absorb carbon dioxide when the trees have leaves. Trees also absorb tiny particles in the atmosphere, which is good for the environment and for our health. All this gives new meaning to the phrase 'Tree of Life'.

And it doesn't stop with plants on the land. Like trees, seagrass growing in shallow water on the coast absorbs a lot of carbon dioxide – 35 times as much as the same area of rainforest. So it is vital to keep our forests, oceans and seas healthy.

10 DESERTS MAKE FOOD FOR FISH

Did you know that a third of all the land on our planet is **desert** – dry sandy or icy regions where almost nothing grows? The driest desert of all is the Atacama in Chile, where in some places no rain has fallen in over four hundred years! Few animals live there because there's hardly any food.

However, deserts are enormously important for life on earth. You might not believe it, but they are a very important food source for everything that lives in the oceans. Tiny creatures that you can't see with the naked eye live in the desert sand and dust. The wind blows the sand and dust into the air, and about a quarter of this dust ends up in the seas and oceans. The tiny creatures become food for sea creatures such as plankton and krill. These are very small shrimp-like animals that some species of whales love to eat. Other fish and sea animals eat krill too. So a minuscule speck of life that can travel on a grain of sand means that there is enough food in the seas and oceans for all other sea creatures. And for humans, too!

one-third of the earth is desert

YUM

THAT'S FISH FOOD!

We can't live on sand, but krill can!

11 HALF THE OXYGEN WE BREATHE COMES FROM THE OCEAN

So if the oceans and seas are full of oxygen, why can't humans can't breathe underwater? Unfortunately, our lungs aren't designed to extract the oxygen, so you'll still need your snorkel. The oxygen is made by **phytoplankton**, tiny algae and bacteria that can only be seen with a microscope. Phytoplankton reproduce in salt water. Usually they can't move on their own, they just float on the sea currents. They use photosynthesis to make energy, absorbing carbon dioxide and releasing oxygen. And plenty of it – in fact, phytoplankton produce as much as half of all the oxygen on our planet! But that's not all. Phytoplankton are also food for animal plankton or **zooplankton**. These are small creatures which, like phytoplankton, can only be seen through a microscope. Zooplankton can move on their own but they cannot swim against the current. They are eaten by small fish and other sea creatures. The fish are then eaten by bigger fish and bigger sea creatures. Some whales also eat zooplankton, as well as krill (tiny shrimps) and their larvae. That's why it's so important that phytoplankton are able to grow. As well as providing a lot of the oxygen needed by living things, they are also the base of underwater food chains. This is why it's vital for us to keep the oceans and seas clean.

OH REALLY?

We can't breathe underwater

> ## BONUS FACT
> Did you know that jellyfish are also a kind of animal plankton? They're made up of 98% water and they aren't strong enough to swim against the current.

phytoplankton and zooplankton

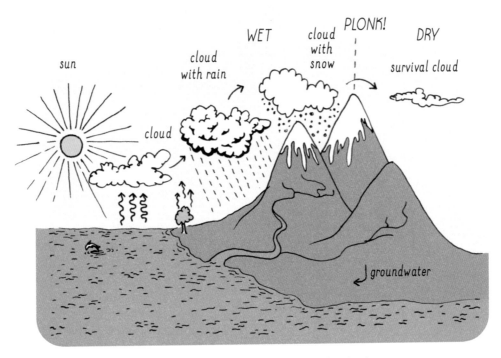

Mountains are an obstacle course for clouds

12 THERE'S A MOUNTAIN IN THE WAY

Deserts are very dry places. That's because very little rain falls. The amount of rain, snow and hail that falls anywhere depends on a lot of things. For example, there might be a mountain in the way.

A **cloud** is a bit like an enormous balloon that's full of water. Water evaporates from oceans, seas, lakes, rivers, woods and forests and rises into the air, where it forms clouds. The wind blows these clouds over the earth's surface until, for instance, they come to a mountain. The mountain makes the clouds rise, cool down and release their water in the form of rain or snow. On the other side of the mountain, much less rain falls. This means that a valley on one side of a mountain can be a lot drier than the valley on the other side. The Scandinavian Mountains, for example, are a range of mountains on the border between

Norway and Sweden. Because of these mountains, it rains more in Norway than in Sweden. Sometimes the valley on the Swedish side gets so little rain that it becomes a desert. The name for this is a **rain shadow**. The Atacama Desert in Chile, Death Valley in the USA and the Gobi Desert in Asia are other examples.

Did you know that not all deserts are hot? The North and South Poles are actually deserts because very little rain falls there, but they are bitterly cold. It is also not true that all deserts are infertile. When a lot of rain falls in some deserts, everything changes as if by magic. Masses of plants suddenly bloom and grow. Unfortunately the soil does not hold the water very well and the plants soon disappear again. But desert sand is a lot more fertile than you think.

the cloud cover is too thick

13 OUR PLANET SHOULD BE CALLED 'WATER', NOT EARTH

If you look at photos of the earth from space, it's pretty clear that we live on a **blue planet**. In fact, it's a bit weird that we call our planet 'earth' and not 'water'! Oceans and seas cover as much as two-thirds of the earth, and the five oceans contain 97% of all the water on the earth. The average depth of the ocean is 4,000 metres, but at its very deepest point, the Mariana Trench in the Pacific Ocean, it's more than 10,000 metres down.

When the sun shines, some of the water evaporates from the ocean. When the water vapour cools down and sometimes freezes, massive clouds are formed. These can rise up to a height of 85 kilometres. The sun's rays bounce off the massive clouds and are sent back into space. By reflecting the sunlight, they stop the earth's temperature from getting too high.

Clouds are blown along by the wind. They carry fresh water all over the world. The water falls in different places in the form of rain, snow or hail. Fresh water is vital for humans, other animals and plants. Living on land would be impossible without it. As well as evaporation, cold and warm currents in the oceans are also important for all living things. They redistribute heat all around the world. The oceans also absorb a lot of heat from the atmosphere.

But when the oceans become too warm, the whole balance is disrupted. Warmer water evaporates more quickly, and this can create powerful hurricanes, for instance. Life under the water also changes when the water warms up. You can read more about that in some of the other sections in this book.

14 ANYONE FOR A GLASS OF GLACIER WATER?

In some places, it's cold and it snows for a very long time. The bottom layer of snow doesn't melt and it is pressed down heavily by the freshly fallen snow. Eventually it becomes solid ice. These large areas of compressed ice and snow are called **glaciers**. They cover about a tenth of the earth's landmass.

Glaciers are usually very big. Even the smallest are as big as a football pitch. The biggest is the Lambert-Fisher Glacier in Antarctica. It is 430 kilometres long and 100 kilometres wide. Glaciers change shape all the time due to gravity and constant movement. You can't see it with the naked eye, but they are constantly moving, just

very slowly. Sometimes a piece breaks off and ends up in the sea. This is called an iceberg. Satellites around the earth are keeping the glaciers under observation, so scientists can see whether they are getting bigger or smaller and how thick the ice layer is.

Glaciers are found almost everywhere on earth. The only continent that doesn't have any is Australia. Occasionally, in places like Ecuador and Mexico, they are packed close together. Glaciers contain a lot of the earth's **fresh water.** Only 2.1% of all the water on earth is fresh, but as much as 69% of it is stored in glaciers. That glass of water you just drank might once have been in a glacier!

melted ice cubes

glacier water anyone?

A GLACIER ON THE ROCKS, PLEASE, SHAKEN NOT STIRRED

15 THE NORTH AND SOUTH POLES ARE OUR PLANET'S AIR CONDITIONING

At the opposite ends of our planet, top and bottom if you like, are the poles. Even though they are the coldest places on the earth, they actually do have seasons.

The **North Pole** is completely made up of sea ice. It's really an enormous frozen ocean, the Arctic Ocean, with no land underneath the ice. The average temperature there is -16°C. In the winter, there is much more sea ice at the North Pole, while in the summer it melts away almost completely. There is land ice on Greenland, but that is not part of the North Pole. It has an ice layer 1,000 to 4,000 metres thick. The North Pole and Greenland are also home to polar bears and seals as well as many other animals.

The **South Pole**, or **Antarctica**, is the coldest place on earth, with an average temperature of -52°C, brrr! It has been frozen for more than 30 million years. The ice is 4,000 metres thick in the middle. In spring, some of it melts and the ocean is filled with marine life such as penguins and whales. That's because algae grows under the sea ice in the winter. Algae is like grass in a meadow and it's the favourite food of tiny shrimps called krill.

As soon as the ice starts to melt, penguins and other animals dive into the water to hunt the krill. Whales swim to the South Pole because they know there is plenty of food there. For most of the humpback whales living in our oceans, the South Pole is a bit like an 'all you can eat' buffet restaurant. The penguins and seals that live there make a tasty meal for killer whales. Albatrosses and other seabirds try to grab a few leftovers after all the other creatures have eaten.

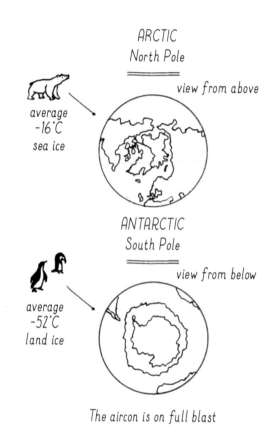

ARCTIC
North Pole

view from above

average
-16°C
sea ice

ANTARCTIC
South Pole

view from below

average
-52°C
land ice

The aircon is on full blast

The North and South Poles also act as enormous white shields that reflect the sun's rays. They are our planet's natural **air conditioning**. If the shields get smaller, they will not be able to reflect as much. The ocean is darker than the ice and therefore it absorbs more heat. Without its air conditioning, the earth won't be able to stay cool enough.

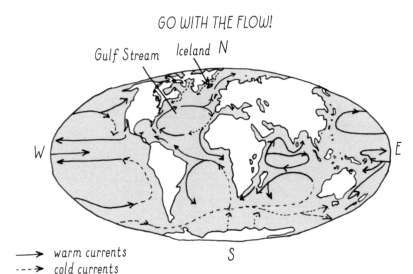

GO WITH THE FLOW!

Gulf Stream   Iceland   N

W

E

S

→ warm currents
---→ cold currents

16 ICELAND ISN'T AS ICY AS YOU THINK

When you hear the name **Iceland** you think of an icy, cold country. Iceland is certainly not far from the North Pole, and in the winter it can get very cold. But did you know that the average temperature in the capital, **Reykjavik**, is 5˚C? That's much higher than in a place like Alaska, a region that is more or less the same distance from the North Pole. The average annual temperature there is just a chilly -3˚C.

Iceland's warmer temperature is due to the **Gulf Stream**, which comes from the Gulf of Mexico and brings with it warm water north and east from the Caribbean. The Irminger Current splits off in the North Atlantic and goes to the south and west coast of Iceland. The current warms the air and that means Iceland is warmer than Alaska. So warm water from the Caribbean controls the average climate of a country in the far north, thousands of miles away.

17 FROM A COUPLE OF THOUSAND TO SEVEN BILLION

Homo sapiens, or in other words humans like you and me, originated about 300,000 years ago. That might seem like a long time, but actually it's quite short when you think that the earth has been around for more than 4.6 billion years. At the beginning, there were not all that many of us, just a couple of hundred thousand. Until 5,000 years ago there were fewer than 20 million people on our planet. The number grew slowly but steadily. In 1500 CE the population was already 500 million. Then 300 years later we passed the billion mark. After that, the increase was fast. In 1900 there were 1.6 billion people and a century later, in 2000, the world population was 6.3 billion. Since then we have reached nearly **8 billion** and every day there are around 227,000 more people. Most live in China (1.39 billion) and India (1.34 billion). Scientists estimate that by the end of this century the world's population will have grown to about 10 billion.

That is an awful LOT of people, and all of them need clean air, drinking water and food. Also, people in rich countries in particular use much more than what the world is able to produce. If everyone in the world consumes as much as we are consuming at the moment, we will no longer be able to produce enough food and dispose of all our waste on a single planet. Unfortunately there isn't another planet that we can move to.

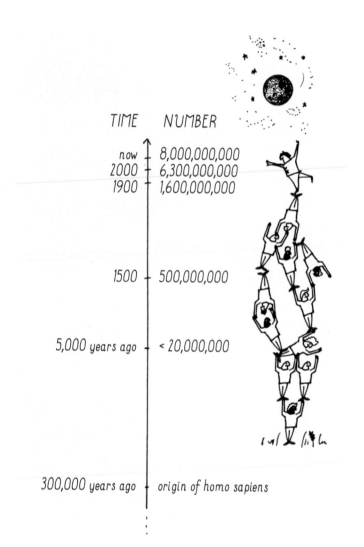

TIME	NUMBER
now	8,000,000,000
2000	6,300,000,000
1900	1,600,000,000
1500	500,000,000
5,000 years ago	< 20,000,000
300,000 years ago	origin of homo sapiens

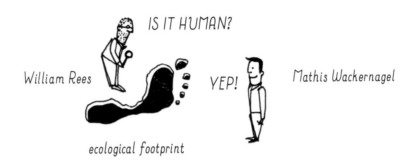

IS IT HUMAN?

William Rees

YEP!

Mathis Wackernagel

ecological footprint

18 WE ARE LIVING (FAR) BEYOND OUR MEANS

In 1992, two Canadian scientists found a way to measure the quantities of raw materials, water and land for food and other products that people and countries needed. They called it the **ecological footprint**. It can be calculated for a single person, a country or a product. The footprint shows the amount of raw materials, water and land for food needed for the life you lead. It is related to what you eat, your transport, your clothes, the way you heat your house, the stuff you buy and so on. It also takes into account how much waste a person or country produces. It's expressed in terms of the areas of land and water surface you would need to produce all your goods and food and dispose of your waste. One hectare is 10,000 square metres, a bit bigger than two football pitches.

If we were to share out all raw materials fairly, each person would be entitled to 1.8 hectares, or a bit less than four football pitches. This is called the **Fair Earth-Share**. But the worldwide average is nearly 2.8 hectares per person. That's mainly because most rich countries live beyond their means. The ecological footprint of an average European is 4.4 hectares, that of the average American as much as 9 hectares. And somebody from the United Arab Emirates has an average footprint of more than 10 hectares. In Africa the average footprint is a lot lower, on average 1.3 hectares per person. So they use less than the two football pitches per person that are available. Are we all going to have to live like people in Africa, then? No, but you can reduce your own footprint a lot by thinking a bit more about some of the things you do.

China, the USA and India have the biggest ecological footprints of all the countries. That's both because a lot of things are made in India and China and because they are very highly populated countries. For people in the United States, their bigger ecological footprint is mainly because people consume a lot of things as well as producing a lot of waste.

You can calculate your ecological footprint at **www.footprintcalculator.org**.

OW!

What is your water footprint?

19 THERE IS VERY LITTLE FRESH WATER IN THE WORLD

As we saw in Fact 13, two-thirds of the earth's surface is covered with water. But most of this is salt water from the oceans and seas. Only 3% of all water is actually fresh water. And of that small amount, we can only use a little bit.

But every living thing in our world – plants, people and other animals – needs fresh water. We need it to drink, to shower, to wash up, to wash our clothes and so on. Farmers need water to grow crops. Factories need water to make all kinds of things. For instance, it takes 2,700 litres of water to make a T-shirt, from the water needed to grow the cotton to the water needed to dye the fabrics. Jeans need as much as 7,500 litres. A kilogram of chicken needs 3,900 litres of water and a kilogram of steak 15,500 litres. Even 10 litres of water are used to make a single sheet of A4 paper.

There is a formula for calculating **water footprints** just as there is for ecological footprints. Firstly, the water that comes out of your tap at home for drinking, washing yourself, cooking, doing the laundry and washing up, cleaning and so on is calculated. Then added to that is the water used to make the goods you buy. These might be made in your own country or in factories far away, often in countries that have much less water than we do. In total, the average British person has a water footprint of approximately 170,000 litres a year.

It is very important to reduce your water footprint. You can do that by keeping tabs on the water you use at home and by thinking carefully when you buy anything.

20 NEARLY ALL MAMMALS ARE FARM ANIMALS

Thousands of years ago, when people first started farming the land, they decided to tame or domesticate animals. It was much easier to milk the cow in the morning or collect eggs from chickens than to go and hunt for meat or have to search for eggs in a nest. Domesticated animals were very useful to humans and now there are huge numbers of them.

- There are as many as 1.5 billion **cows** in the world, a third of them in India. This total includes the 175 million domesticated water buffalo found mainly in Asia.

- The 1.1 billion **sheep** are mostly spread across China, Australia and India. Half of the 1 billion **pigs** are in China. With the 860 million **goats**, 60 million **horses** and 40 million **donkeys**, that comes to 4.7 billion mammals kept as livestock. To say nothing of the 900 million **dogs** and 625 million **cats** that are kept as pets.

- Not only that, but 70% of all the birds in the world are **poultry**, mostly **chickens**. There are estimated to be about 19 billion chickens in the world, about three for every person. Most chickens and eggs are eaten in China, obviously because there are a lot of people there who like chicken.

- All these animals also need a little piece of the earth to live on. And they have to eat. Of all the land we use for farming, more than two-thirds is used to grow animal feed. And of course these animals also need fresh

water (see Fact 19). By eating less meat or no meat at all, you are helping to make sure there is enough land and water left to feed everyone. For instance you could take part in **Meat-Free Monday**, a worldwide movement in which people agree not to eat meat on one day a week. Of course, it doesn't have to be a Monday! If a lot of us keep that up, it will have an enormous impact on the climate and on the environment.

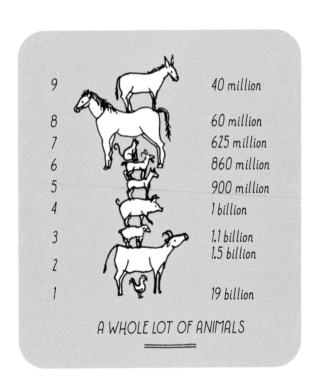

9	40 million
8	60 million
7	625 million
6	860 million
5	900 million
4	1 billion
3	1.1 billion
2	1.5 billion
1	19 billion

A WHOLE LOT OF ANIMALS

21 EVERYTHING IS CONNECTED

Everything on the earth is interconnected. In fact, our planet is actually one huge **ecosystem**. An ecosystem is all the plants, animals and micro-organisms in an environment. They all depend on each other. In fact they couldn't live without one another.

All ecosystems have two parts, a **biotope** and a **community**. The biotope is the environment, or the place where it occurs. The community is everything that grows, flowers and lives there. As well as the forests, oceans, grasslands, coral reefs, deserts and so on in the world, even your back garden and the little pot plants in your living room are ecosystems.

Often it means eating and being eaten. That is called a **food chain**. One organism eats another, and their waste is then food for another one. A forest is full of green organisms: trees, plants, bushes, flowers and mosses. They get their food from the earth. It's provided by the micro-organisms and insects that keep the soil healthy. Worms, beetles, caterpillars and other insects eat the green leaves and rotting wood. Mice love a nice tender beetle and moles are mad about earthworms. Of course they have to make sure they are not on a fox's menu themselves. In the meantime, bees and other pollinators take nectar from flowers and pollinate other plants and trees. There might be deer or wild boar in the forest that like green leaves, chestnuts or acorns. Their droppings make a tasty meal for dung beetles. Birds make nests for their young in the tree branches and fly from there to catch insects.

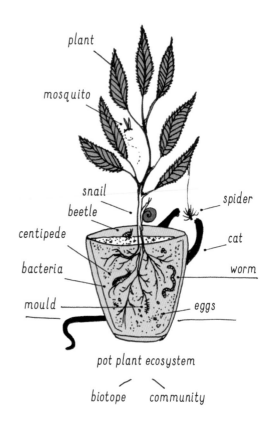

plant
mosquito
snail
beetle
centipede
bacteria
mould
spider
cat
worm
eggs

pot plant ecosystem

biotope   community

And so it goes on. Everything in the forest is connected. If anything in the balance changes, the whole ecosystem changes. When the changes are small, the system can adapt. But big changes, such as the disappearance of certain animals, can cause the whole system to fall apart.

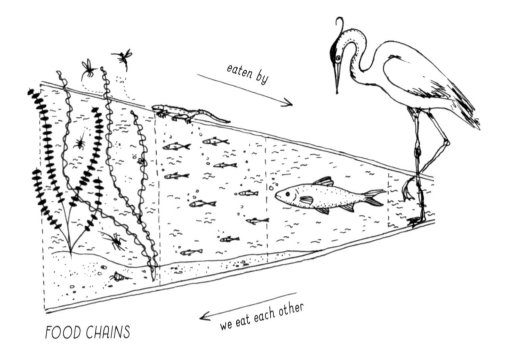

eaten by

we eat each other

FOOD CHAINS

22 YES, WE DO NEED MOSQUITOES

Mosquitoes! You probably don't like them that much. They may wake you up at night with their buzzing and they can give you a nasty, itchy bite. But they are necessary. Their larvae are food for fish and they themselves are a tasty morsel for birds and reptiles.

In every ecosystem there are lots of different kinds of plants and animals. This is called **biodiversity**. 'Bio' means life, 'diversity' means difference or variety. An enormous variety of plants and animals is needed to keep everything working. The various species keep nature balanced. So far scientists have counted about 2 million plant and animal species, but they believe there are many more.

First of all, biodiversity ensures we have enough food. Over 75% of all food crops and as many as 90% of flowering plants need insects and other

creatures to be able to grow. Do you like apples and pears, apricots and peaches, peppers and pumpkins? Well we wouldn't have them if it weren't for animals. More than 200,000 animal species pollinate and fertilize them. Without biodiversity, we would all go hungry.

As well as food, we also get medicines, raw materials for clothes, wood for our houses and fuels from nature. We even depend on biodiversity for the oxygen we breathe. Sadly, more and more animal and plant species are dying out and often human beings are to blame. Once a species has gone, it will never return. The whole ecosystem then becomes much more vulnerable and it can disappear completely. Nature is generous and gives us so much for free, but if we don't protect it, there will be a little bit less every year.

23 WITHOUT CORAL REEFS, THERE'D BE NO LIFE IN THE OCEAN

Coral reefs are a bit like magical kingdoms full of fascinating creatures. These brightly coloured underwater forests are found in the shallow waters of oceans and seas. They are actually made of **coral polyps**. Even though they look like plants, they are actually animals. These living creatures produce chalk and so they are the basis of stony corals. About 1% of the ocean's surface is covered by coral and it plays a vitally important role.

Corals get their bright green, blue, orange or brown colour from the algae they live on.

The algae feed on the carbon dioxide and the waste matter from the coral, while the algae produce the oxygen and food the coral needs. So the algae and the coral need each other. A healthy coral reef provides food for small fish, which graze on the algae. The small fish are in turn food for larger predator fish. The coral also protects the smaller fish. They can hide there and it is also often the place where they lay their eggs. The coral makes sure the newly born fish are not eaten as soon as they are hatched. A quarter of all fish species depend on coral for

WAVE → ← REEF

natural breakwaters

survival. Without coral, fishing boats would not catch nearly as many fish and people would have less to eat. As you can see, coral reefs are vitally important.

But coral does more than that. Coral reefs act as a kind of **breakwater**. They protect the land against flooding and damaging tidal waves. If the coral reefs were to disappear, coastlines would be more vulnerable and much more likely to be damaged during violent sea storms.

So coral reefs are very important ecosystems. But sadly, more and more are disappearing all the time. That endangers not just all marine life but also us humans.

24 SHARKS HELP US SURVIVE

Yes, it's hard to believe, but it's true. Some sharks are true predators. They are at the top of the food chain. That means they eat all kinds of creatures but they themselves have few natural enemies. Only killer whales occasionally dare to attack sharks. These sharks eat other fish, but also sea mammals, birds and carrion (dead animals). There are also giant sharks that just filter plankton and krill from the water. The favourite food of small North Sea sharks is shellfish.

If the sharks were to disappear, the natural environment would quickly go downhill. Often one species of fish becomes dominant and so other species are in danger of dying out. Those other fish species might be important to the coral reef. If they disappear, the coral becomes sick and dies. That's a disaster for the ocean and for us (see Fact 23).

Sharks have been keeping our seas and oceans healthy for more than 450 million years. But sadly, they are now at risk. People catch them for their fins, which are used to make soup, and for their flesh.

It's a fact that every year, around 100 people are attacked by sharks. In 2018, 5 people died after shark attacks. But that's nothing compared with the 100 million sharks that are killed by humans every year. Did you know that 3 sharks die every second? Now you know how important they are to the health and wellbeing of our oceans, can you see why a world without sharks would be such a disaster?

FEELING BAD?

Call Dr Shark

25 ARCHITECTS UNDER THE SEA

Seagrass, cordgrass, mussels and oysters are sometimes called **biobuilders**. Just by being there, they change the environment for the better. They make part of the sea more attractive to other species. In this way, they are similar to coral reefs.

Imagine a bare pebbly beach. At high tide, the plants and animals that grow or live there are crushed between the pebbles. At low tide, they dry out in the sun. **Cordgrass** brings new life. The roots hold the pebbles in place. The cordgrass leaves provide shade from the sun. At high tide, the pebbles no longer roll away and at low tide, the plants and animals no longer dry out. So more organisms can survive on the pebbly beach and there is more food.

Seagrass has a similar effect. It holds back the sand and a thick layer of mud is formed. Small crabs can dig little tunnels in it, which fish can then use to lay their eggs. More species come to live in the places where seagrass grows and biodiversity increases.

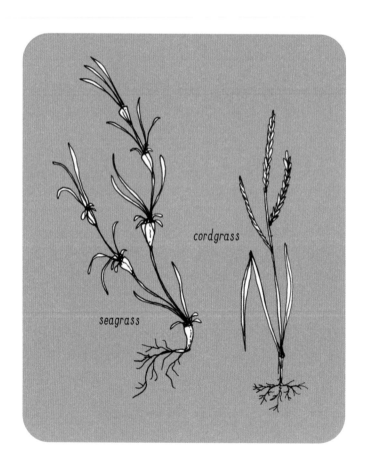

cordgrass

seagrass

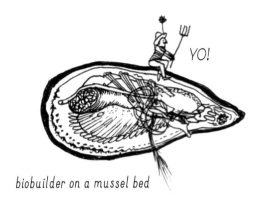

biobuilder on a mussel bed

Mussels and oysters stick together and form large **mussel and oyster beds**. Then, other creatures come along such as snails and shrimps. Fish that like to eat snails and shrimps are also attracted to the beds, together with fish-eating seabirds. The mussels and oysters help keep the water clean. So it is important to have places in our seas where animals, seagrass and cordgrass can grow. They increase biodiversity and keep our seas healthy.

The biobuilders have a hard time. The seas are polluted by chemicals and plastic waste. Fishing nets that are dragged across the seabed break up the plants, grasses and building structures for sea animals. Therefore, they cannot do their work properly any more.

26 CATERPILLARS AND ELEPHANTS BOTH NEED FOREST LEAVES

The Miombo Forest in southern Africa is very special. It lies in a large area with very little food or water. In the spring, **caterpillars** hatch from their eggs and munch on the fresh leaves on the trees. In no time at all the whole forest is bare. The caterpillars grow incredibly fast, getting up to 40 times bigger. At that stage they are a delicacy for animals and birds in the forest.

As soon as the caterpillars have disappeared, the trees have a second growth of leaves. Everything grows and flowers. In the meantime, the area around the forest is completely dry. There is hardly any food or water to be found. So the forest attracts all kinds of mammals, especially **elephants**. They eat the leaves and branches in the forest. In fact an adult elephant can easily eat 200 kilograms of food in a day! That opens up the dense forest, which is good for other animals such as deer and antelopes. African wild dogs also like the open forest, where it is easy for them to hunt their prey. They can make their underground dens in the forest. Their young are born there and the adults can teach them what they need to know in order to survive.

So an unlikely relationship between tiny caterpillars and huge elephants helps make sure the forest remains healthy and is a refuge for many other animals. This is a good example of how everything is interconnected.

the hornbill preserves the forest

27 POO KEEPS THE FOREST HEALTHY

We weren't going to mention it, but it's actually quite important. Animals do provide a lot of **manure**! That's certainly true. And animals provide a lot more than that. In fact, the forest couldn't survive without them.

We're taking you now on a journey to the Western Ghats, a mountain range in India with various kinds of rainforest. It's home to nearly 140 species of mammals, more than 500 species of birds, many butterfly species, 200 species of reptiles and 180 species of amphibians. Many of these species are only found in the Western Ghats and they are endangered.

Among the many animals living in the forests are monkeys. They are mad about fruit and they gorge on it. When the fruit seeds, undigested or semi-digested, are excreted, new trees can grow from them. Unfortunately the monkeys don't travel all that far, so the seeds are only spread around their area. Luckily, the forest is also home to magnificent birds called hornbills that love figs. The fig trees in the forest can attract hundreds of birds. They eat the figs and then fly across the forest. On the way, they might drop a digested fig containing fig seeds and seeds from other fruit trees. These can germinate far from where they were eaten. In this way, the forest animals help the forest to survive and spread. Clever, isn't it?

28 THERE IS NO PLANET B

You might have seen this slogan on placards at climate demonstrations. It basically means that the earth is the only planet in the solar system on which humans can live comfortably. The earth's temperature is just right, there is oxygen to breathe, we have water to drink, we are protected against the sun's rays and we have enough food. And besides, everything looks really good. Why would you want to live on any other planet? No other planet is this human-friendly.

Take **Mercury**, for example. The daytime temperature can be 465°C, but at night it cools down to -185°C. That is not exactly pleasant for people or animals. What's more, there is no liquid water and no atmosphere. The ultraviolet light from the sun would shine straight onto the surface and we would not survive for very long. How about **Venus?** No, it's very hot, around 475°C, and there are clouds of sulphur drifting across it. Pretty unhealthy, in our opinion. **Mars**, on the other hand, is too cold. Liquid water has been found, but it is in a large underground lake. And the atmosphere lets too much ultraviolet sunlight through. So not really an option. Meanwhile, **Jupiter**, **Saturn**, **Uranus** and **Neptune** are gas giants that are a very long way from the sun. It would be impossible to live there.

Of course, some scientists are looking for ways of moving to another planet, and maybe they will find a planet on which some form of life is possible. But every living thing on earth has adapted to our planet over millions of years. It would be much more difficult to survive anywhere else. So it's more sensible to think of ways that we can make sure the planet we have stays habitable.

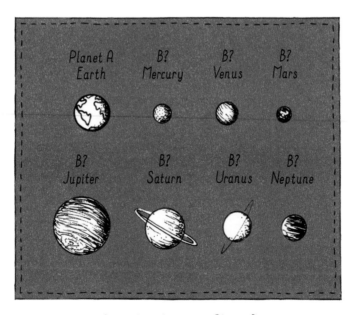

Sorry, but there is no Planet B

29 FLOWERS NEED BEES AND SO DO WE

BZZZ

Bees need flowers, flowers need bees!

You've probably heard grown-ups use the expression 'the birds and the bees'? Basically, it's a roundabout way of talking about where babies come from. In fact **honey bees**, **bumblebees**, **wasps** and other buzzing insects are an essential part of nature. They are needed to pollinate many of the crops we eat. If you want to eat apples, pears, raspberries, blackberries, peppers, courgettes, pumpkins and loads of other kinds of fruit and vegetables, you need a lot of buzzing insects. Bees and wasps in search of nectar are attracted by flowers and blossom. They crawl deep into the flower to get at the sweetness. At that point, grains of pollen stick to their bodies. When they land on another flower, the pollen falls off. That fertilizes the plant and means that fruit can grow on it. So it is thanks to bees and other buzzing insects that we can eat all these delicious fruits and vegetables.

parts of a flower

Honey bees make honey from nectar. It takes the nectar from as many as 16 million flowers to make one kilogram of honey. The bees use the honey themselves to survive through the winter, but they don't mind sharing it with us. The workers are busy every day collecting the precious substance and at the same time they pollinate thousands of flowers. An average hive contains about 20,000 bees.

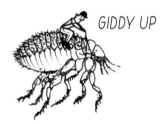

GIDDY UP

this 'mite bee' the biggest threat to bees

Sadly, the bee population is in decline. In Europe nearly a third of all beehives have died. This is partly due to the **Varroa mite**, a parasite which infects and kills them. But humans are also responsible. Bees find fewer and fewer plants containing the nectar they need. Besides that, farmers and gardeners often use toxic substances or **pesticides** to kill harmful insects. Unfortunately these are also bad for bees. Without bees, not only is there no honey, but most of our other food disappears too. And we don't want that, do we?

Farmers are now realizing more and more that they need bees. They are using fewer or different pesticides, and are looking for little spots or corners in their fields where wildflowers can grow, specially for bees. Councils are having verges mown or trimmed less so that more wildflowers grow and beehives are being set up in lots of different places, even on flat roofs in towns. Everyone is trying to increase the bee population again. So if a bee buzzes past you, give it a wave instead of waving it away.

2

THE CLIMATE KEEPS CHANGING ...
SO THE EARTH DOES TOO

30 IN 4.6 BILLION YEARS THE CLIMATE HAS ALREADY SEEN MANY CHANGES

Our planet is a staggering 4.6 billion years old! So the earth is a lot older than the human race, which has only been around for a mere 300,000 years.

- The climate has already undergone many changes. At times our planet was almost completely covered in snow and ice. About 700 million years ago it looked like an enormous snowball hovering in space. The average temperature was -45°C, so it was bitterly cold. Nothing much could live on it then.

- At other times the earth was much warmer than it is now. Sometimes, for instance, there was no ice at the poles. Palm trees even grew at the North Pole (see Fact 31).

- About 2.7 million years ago, **ice ages** or **glacial periods**, which lasted about 100,000 years, began to alternate with **interglacial periods**, which lasted about 10,000 years. The last ice age lasted until 12,000 years ago. Then an interglacial period, the **Holocene**, started. We are still living in it now.

- Most changes in the climate were completely natural. You can read more about them in the sections that follow.

'old' earth
4.6 billion years

WHAT?

'not so old' human
I'm 300,000 years young!

31 55 MILLION YEARS AGO, YOU COULD SUNBATHE AT THE POLES

Did you know that 55 million years ago the average temperature on earth was about 25°C? Even in winter, the poles didn't freeze. You could lie under palm trees and animals that were the ancestors to hippos and crocodiles were walking around. Researchers still don't know why the earth was so warm then. In 20,000 years (a very short time in the earth's history) it warmed up as much as five degrees. Maybe the many volcanoes that were erupting everywhere had something to do with it. Or perhaps it suddenly got warmer because of something happening deep in the oceans. The ocean bed was full of the rotting remains of plants and animals. It was icy cold. But for all sorts of reasons the earth warmed up a bit and so did the seabed.

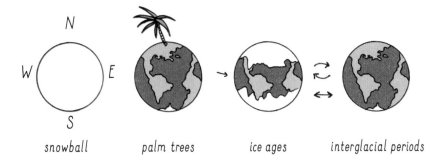

snowball   palm trees   ice ages   interglacial periods

The remains of the plants and animals released a gas called **methane**. It rose to the surface in large air bubbles. At the surface they burst. The methane ended up in the atmosphere, where it mixed with carbon dioxide, resulting in a very warm period. A greenhouse effect was created.

It stayed warm on the earth for 20 million years! Then 35 million years ago South America and Australia broke off from the South Pole and drifted away. The water at the South Pole circulated. No warm water flowed in, so everything quickly cooled down. That created a solid ice cap, which is still there. The rest of the ocean also cooled down and a couple of severe ice ages started. So that was the end of sunbathing at the North Pole!

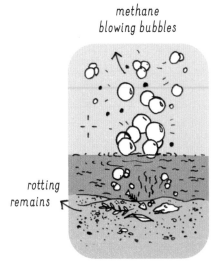

methane
blowing bubbles

rotting
remains

It's 25°C and sunny!

32 MIRROR, MIRROR, AT THE POLE

It's a scorchingly hot day in summer, so hot your ice cream melts before you have a chance to eat it. What would you rather wear, light or dark clothes? We think light-coloured clothes are cooler. That's because they reflect the sunlight more, so you don't feel so hot. Dark clothes absorb the sun's rays and you start to sweat. How much something reflects the sun is called the **albedo**.

Clouds, snow, ice, water and all other mirror surfaces are **reflective**. Fresh snow and ice have an albedo of 80 to 95%. If the snow melts or becomes dirty, the figure drops to between 40 and 70%. Clouds have an albedo of 40 to 90%, depending on the thickness of the cloud, the angle at which the sun's rays fall on the cloud, the size of the drops and whether the cloud contains rain

or ice. The rest of the earth does not reflect so well. Water has an albedo between 10 and 60%. That partly depends on the angle at which the sun's rays fall on the water and how rough the sea is. If the whole earth was covered with snow and ice, the albedo would be 84%. If the earth was completely covered with trees, with no snow or ice, it would have a 14% albedo.

You can work out for yourself why the earth gets warmer when the ice melts. Large areas of water and land are uncovered. Think of Greenland, Antarctica and glaciers high in the mountains. Those areas are darker and they cannot reflect the sun's rays as well. So the seawater warms up and that can lead to major climate changes.

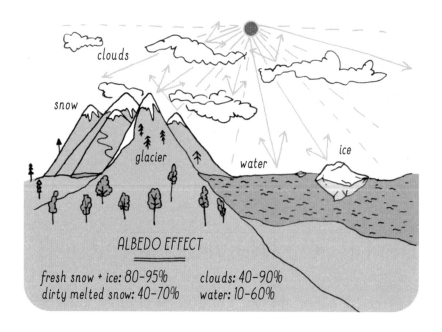

clouds

snow

glacier

water

ice

ALBEDO EFFECT

fresh snow + ice: 80-95%   clouds: 40-90%
dirty melted snow: 40-70%   water: 10-60%

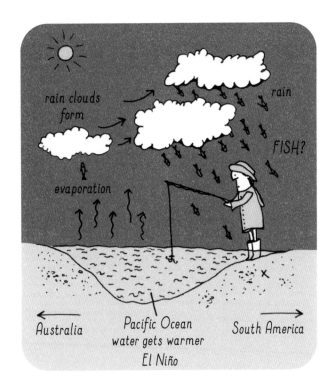

33 EL NIÑO AND THE CLIMATE

Occasionally, something unusual happens in the Pacific Ocean on the west coast of South America. The normally cool seawater warms up. The fishermen there call that **El Niño**, which means 'little boy' or 'Baby Jesus', because it mostly reaches its peak around Christmas time. The warm current has a massive impact on the weather and the environment.

Fishermen dread the arrival of **El Niño**. There is less food for the fish in warm water. In an El Niño year, fishermen catch much less fish than at other times. It also affects the climate all over the world. The warm water evaporates more quickly and an enormous amount of rain falls on places that are normally dry. That causes floods and mudslides in the South American Andes Mountains and houses are washed away. The effects are also felt on the

other side of the ocean. It causes severe drought in Australia, Indonesia and South Asia, leading to widespread forest fires and failed harvests.

Scientists never know exactly when El Niño will occur. On average it recurs every three to seven years. The last one was in 2019.

The opposite can also happen. Then we call it La Niña (which means 'little girl'). At that time the seawater on the Pacific coast is colder than usual. That can cause more droughts in some places and more hurricanes in the Caribbean. La Niña generally has a less serious impact than El Niño.

34 VOLCANOES AND METEORITES

In a **volcanic eruption** a lot of stuff from inside the earth gets blown out. These eruptions have a big impact on climate. As well as lava flowing out, a thick cloud of dust and sulphur ends up in the atmosphere, blocking out the sunlight. The sun's rays aren't able to reach the earth and it gets a lot colder. Also, more carbon dioxide is released in the eruption and life on earth becomes very difficult for living things. The biggest volcanic eruption ever was from **Mount Tambora** on the Indonesian island of Sumbawa. But even smaller volcanoes such as Mount Vesuvius in Sicily, Laki in Iceland and Pinatubo in the Philippines noticeably changed the climate when they erupted.

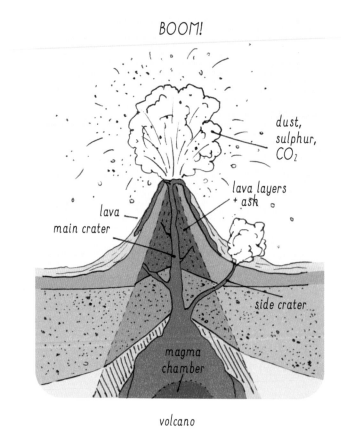

BOOM!

dust, sulphur, CO_2

lava layers + ash

lava

main crater

side crater

magma chamber

volcano

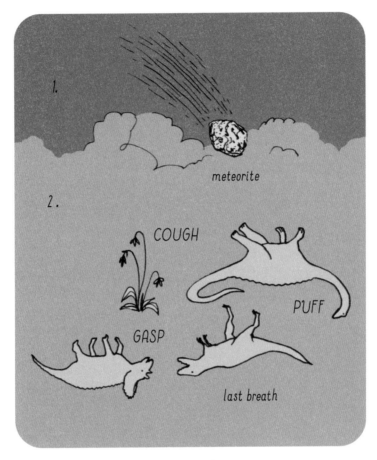

the end of the dinosaurs

Sometimes, the disaster comes from space. A falling **meteorite** can change the climate in the blink of an eye. Think of the meteorite that fell in Mexico in the time of the **dinosaurs**. It stirred up such an enormous cloud of dust that nothing on earth could grow any more. Plants began to die, which meant that plant-eating dinosaurs had nothing to eat and they starved. And without plant-eating dinosaurs, there was nothing for meat-eating dinosaurs to eat. Dinosaurs had survived on earth for 165 million years, but they were quickly wiped out by the climate change that followed.

gobbledygook? *

EH?

* *what's for dinner?*

35 CLIMATE CHANGE MADE PEOPLE START TALKING

The earth hasn't always been the same temperature. The period from 5.3 to 2.6 million years ago was the **Pliocene Epoch**. At that time the average temperature was 3˚C warmer. That also made the sea level rise. Because of the warmer climate Africa became very dry. That was hard for the early hominids who lived there, because they found less and less food. There were fewer animals to hunt and less fruit grew on the plants. Sometimes there was so little to eat that they just had to move somewhere else.

But there was one good thing about the food shortage. People were forced to **communicate** better with each other. That was the only way they could make it clear where there was still something to eat, or whether it was time to move to a place where they could find food and water.

So the warmer climate meant that the early hominids had to adapt to the new, much drier environment and they started 'talking' to each other more. Their brain volume grew and they got a lot smarter.

Because of the drought these early humans started hunting more, since there was less and less food they could pick. Meat was tasty but it was a bit heavy on the stomach. People soon realized that a piece of meat was easier to digest if you cooked it first. It wasn't long before they found out how to start fires themselves. So the discovery of language and fire were indirect consequences of the warmer climate.

36 BECAUSE OF CLIMATE CHANGE, HUMANS SPREAD TO EVERY CONTINENT

Many years ago, Africa was so dry that nearly all of its forests had disappeared. All that was left was a huge grassy area with a few bushes and trees. People walked upright in the long grass so they could keep a lookout. There might be juicy prey for them to hunt or even a predator they needed to hide from.

Then, about 1.8 million years ago, the earth started to cool down. An ice age started. The poles kept getting bigger. It snowed all the time. The snow settled and was compressed into a solid mass. The land ice and sea ice grew quickly. It was so cold that the ice didn't melt in the spring and summer. So no water flowed back to the oceans and seas and the water level fell. At that time the water was as much as 120 metres lower than it is now. Parts of the earth that always had water dried out. That gave early humans a chance to go off exploring. They trekked across the dry seabeds from Africa to the rest of the world.

Because of this climate change, early humans discovered the world and settled all over it. But these were hard times. Many of our ancient ancestors did not survive the ice ages. Our early ancestors could only survive in a part of Africa where there was still food. Only people who could think ahead and were very smart survived. We call them **homo sapiens**, which means 'wise men', although it's safe to say there were wise women too! They are our distant ancestors.

WOW!

Now we can spend more time
with the kids!

37 CLIMATE CHANGE TURNED PEOPLE INTO FARMERS

Brrr! It's true to say that long **ice ages** were always difficult times for humankind. The last one began about 117,000 years ago and ended 12,000 years ago. It was still a while before the earth warmed up enough, but 11,000 years ago, life started to get easier. We call this the **Holocene** period. Temperatures rose. Everything on earth grew and bloomed abundantly. This was good for hunter-gatherers. They could pick their food from the trees or the earth. And there were more animals to hunt.

With a full stomach, people could think about having babies. The population grew quickly. People started living in larger groups and they established communities. But then the climate changed. For a thousand years, the average temperature was much colder. This meant there was less food. Luckily, people had now become smarter. They had discovered that some seeds grew again if they were scattered on the earth. Some people started experimenting with seeds and other crops. They found out what kind of soil these grew well in and how to look after them properly. So they became less dependent on plants that grew naturally. They also learned how to preserve the things they grew so that they had food for times when little or nothing grew. Climate change turned people into **farmers**. The better they could work the land, the more food there was. This also gave people a chance to focus on other things, such as inventing, reading and writing, or building better houses.

38 CLIMATE CHANGE DESTROYED GREAT CIVILIZATIONS

The climate is always changing, whether we like it or not. Ice ages alternate with warmer periods. The last great ice age ended about 12,000 years ago. Since then, the climate has remained fairly stable. There was only one short ice age between 1200 and 1850.

The climate does not change in the same way everywhere. For instance, sometimes it gets drier in a certain place. If there is a large community living there, it becomes hard for them to survive because they can't harvest enough food. The **Maya** people of South America lived well for 3,000 years. They grew all kinds of crops and the population increased. Large cities sprung up. But around 900 CE it all went wrong. The region where the Maya lived was hit by drought. The harvests failed. There was not enough food or water for everyone. The Maya tried to take more land from other peoples, but that too was unsuccessful. Their civilization was eventually destroyed by climate change.

I'M TOO HOT

ME TOO

Mayan man

The same happened to other great civilizations. When people use up too many of their food and water sources, things can go wrong. We are seeing that happen all over the world now. Around 20 to 30% of all animal species are threatened with extinction. If the sea level rises too much, cities will be flooded. A temperature rise of a couple of degrees can lead to a massive drought, so that in some places there will not be enough to eat.

3

THE EARTH IS GETTING HOTTER

39 THE STORY OF THE BOILED FROG

We're definitely not suggesting you try this, but rumour has it that if you throw a frog into a pan of boiling water, it jumps straight out again. But if you put the frog into cold water and warm the water slowly until it starts boiling, the frog just sits there calmly. Eventually the poor frog is boiled alive without even realizing it. The climate is a bit like that. We've known for ages that the earth is getting hotter, but we just did nothing. In 1956, an American newspaper wrote that **fossil fuels** were responsible for higher temperatures. It warned that **greenhouse gases** were a threat to life on earth. More than 60 years later, little has been done worldwide to stop this. In fact, we're producing more carbon dioxide than before.

Why is this? Climate change is slow and it does not have the same effects everywhere. Sometimes the short-term effects are actually positive (see Fact 43). Who doesn't like a nice warm summer? Things would be different if the changes happened quickly and we felt the effects right away. Then we would probably try to act immediately.

Climate change is not the fault of one or two people. We all play a part. Many people do not see it as their problem. They don't think one person can do anything about it. Besides that, there are so many serious problems we need to find solutions for: hunger, poverty, environmental pollution and more. Sometimes people just find the climate too much to deal with.

Finally, people generally don't like change. And the climate problem is something that calls for a lot of changes if we want future generations to be able to live comfortably.

Luckily, there are more and more people who want to do something. For instance **Greta Thunberg**, the Swedish girl who started by striking on one day a week. Now thousands of schoolchildren all over the world are following her example and Greta is invited to all kinds of top-level climate conferences. She's a bit like the frog that jumped out of the water and is warning us all.

WHAT A LOVELY, WARM BATH!

It's getting hotter!

summer   winter

40 IT HAS NEVER BEEN SO HOT

The World Meteorological Organization (WMO) measures the earth's temperature. It gets the information from scientific bodies such as the European Centre for Medium-Range Weather Forecasts (ECMWF), the National Aeronautics and Space Administration (NASA) and the National Oceanic and Atmospheric Administration (NOAA). The ECMWF uses measurements by the **European Space Agency (ESA)**, which has the best satellites for monitoring the earth's climate and environment from space. According to WMO calculations, the average temperature in 2019 was 1.1°C higher than the average between 1850 and 1900. The years 2015 to 2019 were the hottest since temperatures have been measured and recorded.

Well, 1.1°C doesn't sound like much, does it? No, but it's definitely a move in the wrong direction. If we carry on as we are and produce just as many greenhouse gases, we can expect the earth to be 2.6 to 4.8°C hotter by the year 2100. The temperature will not rise the same amount everywhere. The area around the North Pole will get particularly warm, melting the polar ice. The WMO predicts that we will have extremely high temperatures more often but we might also get very cold winters.

Luckily, this doesn't have to happen. If we manage to reduce greenhouse gas emissions by 40 to 70% by 2050, the temperature rise would be limited to between 0.3 and 1.7°C. By around 2100, there should not be any more greenhouse gas emissions. But those are very bold aims. So it's high time for the government and businesses to make a start.

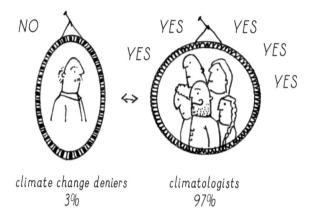

climate change deniers
3%

climatologists
97%

41 THERE ARE PEOPLE WHO DON'T BELIEVE IN CLIMATE CHANGE

Some people claim that climate change is a myth. Or rather, they think climate change has nothing to do with human beings. They say the earth has always got hotter and colder. Those people are called **climate change deniers**. Often they don't believe that people are able to change anything as big as the climate.

We do know now that the average temperature on the earth is rising. Nearly all climatologists (more than 97%) believe that global warming is caused mainly by human activity. The information they collect is coordinated by the **Intergovernmental Panel on Climate Change (IPCC)**, an international group of experts from universities, research centres, environmental groups, businesses and other organizations. The IPCC does not do any research itself but it evaluates all the information it receives and uses it to draw up reports.

We now know from all that research that the burning of oil, gas and coal since the industrial revolution has played a big part in climate change. Climate scientists are still debating how much the temperature will rise, what influence rising temperatures will have on sea levels and what effects climate change will have on humans. Some scientists are fairly pessimistic. Others think that humankind is clever enough to come up with solutions to the problem. In any case, it is becoming one of humanity's biggest challenges.

42 CLIMATOLOGY IS A JOB

People have always been fascinated by the weather and climate. At first it was chemists, physicists, geologists, astronomers and even mathematicians who studied weather and climate. Now there are also people who call themselves **climatologists**. They carry out research into how and why the climate behaves in a certain way. A climate researcher wants to know why the average temperature on earth rises or falls, why it rains more in some places and less in others, why it is windier and there are more storms. They look at changes in the past to see if we can learn lessons from them.

Other climatologists study deforestation or the melting of the icecaps. To discover the effects of climate change, they come up with various experiments and try to make scientifically based predictions.

Climatologists will have an important job in the future. The government and quite a number of companies want to hire specialists in climate and environmental sciences to find solutions to their problems. You might soon be one of them!

biologist

physicist

mathematician

astronomer

geologist

chemist

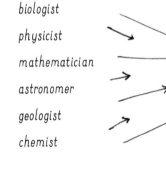

climatologist

43 PROFESSOR ARRHENIUS THOUGHT A WARMER CLIMATE MIGHT BE BETTER

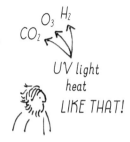

CO_2 O_3 H_2

UV light
heat
LIKE THAT!

physicist
John Tyndall

In the 19th century, scientists discovered that greenhouse gases and temperature were connected. In 1859, the Irish physicist **John Tyndall** proved that gases such as carbon dioxide, hydrogen and ozone absorbed infrared light, which is actually heat. Then, in 1896, the Swedish scientist **Svante Arrhenius** calculated how much warmer the earth would become if there was twice as much carbon dioxide in the atmosphere. At the time, the higher emissions were mostly caused by burning coal, a fossil fuel that is still used to heat houses and generate electricity.

Arrhenius worked out that the temperature would rise a lot if we pumped more carbon dioxide into the atmosphere. He didn't think that was such a bad idea. It would make the climate warmer in cold areas and so more pleasant. It would be easier to grow different kinds of crops, harvests would be bigger and that was good for farmers and people in colder areas.

He did not know then that climate change could also cause a lot of problems, such as drought in some places and floods in others. He may have thought differently if he had known.

IT'S NICE AND WARM FOR EVERYONE!

AAAH!

Svante Arrhenius

44 A VOLCANO IS A GOOD PLACE TO MEASURE CARBON DIOXIDE

Mauna Loa is a volcano on the island of Hawaii in the middle of the Pacific Ocean. It is the biggest volcano in the world, towering up more than 4,000 metres above sea level. At 3,397 metres, there is an observatory where the carbon dioxide level is measured, because the air is very clean there. There is no traffic in the area and no factories producing carbon dioxide.

The American chemist **Charles David Keeling** started measuring carbon dioxide on Mauna Loa in 1958. He recorded the figures on a graph and they formed a curve, which we now call the **Keeling Curve**. The horizontal axis shows the time in years, the vertical axis the amount of carbon dioxide measured. You can see an upward line since 1958, varying according to the season. The volcano is above the equator in the northern hemisphere. There you have a clear difference between winter and summer. In winter, CO_2 levels increase because there are no leaves on the trees. The spring always shows a peak. That is when the carbon dioxide in the air is at its highest level. In summer the amount of carbon dioxide drops again because the plants and trees then absorb more gas. You can see clearly from the Keeling Curve that every year the spring peak is higher than in the previous year. So year by year there is more carbon dioxide in the air. Climatologists see that as a dangerous trend. It means that the average temperature on earth is rising, which is not good news.

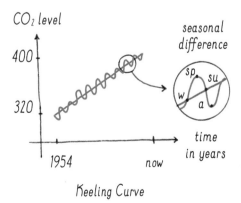

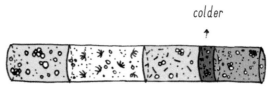

colder
↑

ice nucleus

45 WE'RE LIVING ABOVE THE CRITICAL CO₂ THRESHOLD

The carbon dioxide level is expressed in **parts per million**, or **ppm**. In 1750 the carbon dioxide level was 280 ppm. That means that there were 280 parts (or molecules) of carbon dioxide in 1 million air particles. So 280 out of 1 million isn't a lot, but it has serious effects if it increases.

Know-it-alls point out that there were no measuring stations in 1750. Well, that's true. But climatologists have drilled 'old' ice out of icecaps and glaciers. These long tubes of ice contain air bubbles. By analysing the air bubbles, researchers can find out what was in the atmosphere up to a million years ago. We know from examining the ice that the highest concentration of carbon dioxide (400 ppm) dates from about 5 million years ago. At that time it was 4 to 5 degrees warmer than now and the sea level was 40 metres higher. That was followed by ice ages and the carbon dioxide level fell to 180 ppm. In the last 10,000 years, the content stayed fairly stable at around 280 ppm. Human development continued. Particularly since the 18th century we see the carbon dioxide level slowly but surely rising. When measurements started on Mauna Loa (see Fact 44), the carbon concentration was 320 ppm.

On 9 May 2013, the concentration went above 400 ppm for the first time. Scientists call this the 'critical threshold'. If the carbon dioxide in the atmosphere remains at that level, the earth will go back to how it was 5 million years ago. Since 2015, we have always been above the critical 400 ppm threshold and the CO₂ level continues to rise by 2 ppm per year. You can see why climatologists are trying to raise the alarm!

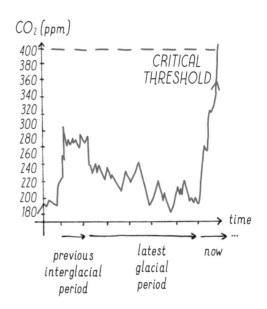

46 A FOREST THE SIZE OF SEVENTEEN FOOTBALL PITCHES VANISHES EVERY MINUTE

A third of the land on earth is covered in woodland, some of it tropical rainforest like the Amazon rainforest in South America, the rainforest in Africa's Congo basin and the South-East Asian rainforest. There is also the taiga, a vast forest stretching across Russia, northern Europe and part of the United States. Trees feed on carbon dioxide, storing it in their trunks and roots and in the soil (see Fact 9).

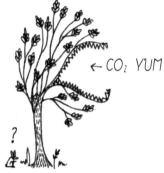

← CO_2 YUM

CO_2-eating trees

Sadly, all those forests are quickly disappearing. Every year 6.5 million hectares of natural woodland is cut down worldwide. That's equivalent to 17 football pitches every minute! The trees are felled to make room for agricultural land, roads and houses or to dig out underground mines. Besides that, large areas of woodland are burnt down in forest fires. Often the fires are started to make more room for agriculture. That means that less carbon dioxide can be absorbed and large ecosystems disappear. Animals lose their habitats and become extinct. All kinds of plant species disappear, never to return. With every forest that disappears, a part of life on our planet is lost, probably for ever.

one-third forested | two-thirds not forested

land on the earth

47 IT STARTED WITH A REVOLUTION

The problems we are facing today started with the **industrial revolution**. The first steam engine was invented around 1606. The energy that drove it came from burning coal. It wasn't long before steam trains started running, steamships crossed the oceans, people worked in factories and iron and steel were mass-produced. Until then, people had got their energy from burning wood or dried animal dung. For work they mostly used human or animal muscle power. There were also water- and wind-powered mills, to grind their corn.

But the discovery of fossil fuels, first **coal** and later **petrol** and **gas**, changed all that. The fuels were the remains of plants, trees and animals that had been underground for millions of years. They were buried under masses of earth, which had compressed them at high temperatures.

A BRILLIANT INVENTION!

steam engine

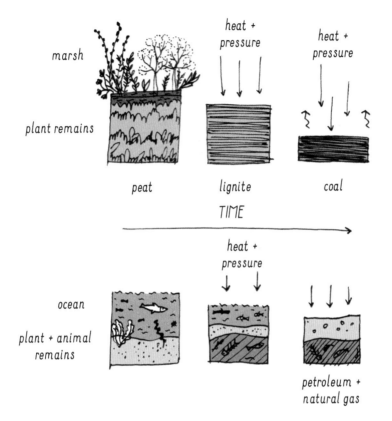

marsh

plant remains

peat

heat + pressure

lignite

heat + pressure

coal

TIME

ocean

plant + animal remains

heat + pressure

heat + pressure

petroleum + natural gas

Coal, petrol and gas were formed deep in the earth. All the carbon dioxide those plant and animal remains had ever absorbed was buried deep underground. When it was brought back to the surface and burned, a lot more CO_2 was released into the air than ever before. Since the industrial revolution we can see that the **carbon dioxide** level has kept rising. And 83 to 95% of the increase is due to the burning of oil, coal and gas. Admittedly fossil fuels have given people a much more comfortable life. We were able to heat our houses, drive cars and even fly to the moon. We know now that there are no 'clean' fossil fuels. Coal causes the most pollution, but oil and gas are not 'clean' either. So we urgently need to look for alternatives.

exploration ship with mini-mast

48 WE NEVER THOUGHT WOOD COULD RUN OUT

We humans are naturally curious, and in the 15th and 16th centuries, people set out to explore the world. They wanted to know what lands lay on the other side of the great ocean. To do that they needed ships, which were made of **wood**. At that time there were only sailing ships, so they had to have masts. Only tall, strong trees were suitable for the purpose. Everything was fine to start with, but then people noticed that really big trees were getting harder to find. In Italy, Portugal and Spain they soon ran out of trees that were big enough. After that they had their ships built in the colonies they had just conquered. Wood is not unlimited and we have already used a lot of it. Three quarters of China was once forested. Now there is barely 5% left. In the USA, only 7% of the virgin forest remains. More than half of the **tropical rainforest** has gone. It takes a long time for forests to grow back again. If we stop deforestation now, we can reduce carbon dioxide emissions by a fifth. In the next 50 years we also need an intensive global effort to plant new trees. That will help to slow down global warming.

49 WALK OR CYCLE TO AVOID EMITTING CARBON DIOXIDE

Do you always walk or cycle? Well done! Then you're not emitting carbon dioxide, apart from the little bit you breathe out. Most motorized transport does emit carbon dioxide, but not all the same amount.

When you take the **train**, you emit 28 grams of CO_2 per kilometre. On the **bus** the emission goes up to 68 grams per kilometre and on a **motor scooter up** to 72 grams. In a small **family car** you emit an average of 104 grams per kilometre, and with a large car 158 grams. Of course it depends what car you drive. Cars running on petrol, diesel or gas all emit greenhouse gases. The more they use, the greater the emissions. Basically an **electric car** does not emit greenhouse gases, provided that it runs on renewable green energy such as wind or solar power. And of course a lot of carbon dioxide is emitted in the manufacture of those cars. **Aircraft** create a lot of emissions, about 285 grams per kilometre per passenger.

There are lots of websites where you can calculate the emissions created by a journey by car, train or aeroplane. This might be a useful way to find out if you want to become a world traveller!

BONUS FACT

Over half the car journeys we make are shorter than 5 kilometres. Maybe you could see whether your school is close enough to home for you to walk or cycle there, or go by public transport.

transport	emission level
walking	0g CO_2
kick scooter	0g CO_2
skateboard	0g CO_2
roller skates	0g CO_2
train	28g CO_2
bus	68g CO_2
motor scooter	72g CO_2
small car	104g CO_2
large car	158g CO_2
aeroplane	285g CO_2

50 FLYING CAUSES POLLUTION

Would it surprise you to know that only twenty out of every hundred people have ever been on an aeroplane? They are mainly people from rich countries. Maybe you're one of them? **Flying** is fun, but unfortunately it's also really bad for the environment. Especially during take-off, when planes emit huge amounts of pollutants, including **carbon dioxide** and **nitrous oxides** (NO_x), which form ozone. It's estimated that about 348 billion kilograms of kerosene, the aircraft fuel made of oil, were used in 2019.

The number of flights is on the rise. In 1950, 31 million people made a plane journey. By 1986 that had already gone up to 960 million! And in 2012 as many as 3 billion passengers travelled by air. Half of the passengers are tourists. About 45% of all flights are over distances of less than 500 kilometres. The number of freight transport flights has also risen more than 70% over a ten-year period.

Is it a bird, or is it a plane?

Airlines expect the number of passengers to carry on growing. In 2019, there were already 4.5 billion passengers a year. And more freight will be transported by air as well. If that's true, all efforts to reduce carbon emissions in other areas are pointless. Since we can't grow our own wings, we have to look for creative solutions to limit flying or make it more climate-friendly.

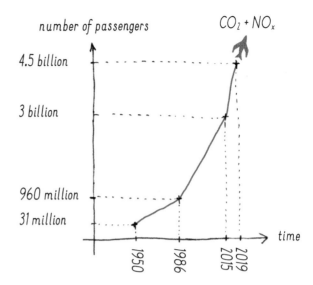

51 COWS BURP AND FART TOO MUCH

Cows are lovely animals aren't they, but they do have a big problem. Cows – and all other ruminants – are very flatulent. What's more, they love to burp. When they fart and burp they emit a lot of **methane** (CH_4). One cow produces between 100 to 300 litres of CH_4 a day. Methane is a dangerous greenhouse gas. It's 34 times stronger than carbon dioxide, but it doesn't stay in the air for as long. It's emitted during oil and gas exploitation, when tropical rainforests are burned and when ruminants fart and burp!

In Fact 20, we learned that there are 1.5 billion cows in the world. Together they emit 10 to 15% of greenhouse gases, 40% from their **burps** and **farts**. The other 60% is mainly carbon dioxide and some nitrous oxide from fertilizer spread over the pastures the cows graze on, animal transport, the treatment of manure and so on.

Obviously, we can't ask cows to stop burping and farting. That wouldn't be good for them. So we have to make sure they burp and fart less. Amongst other things farmers are experimenting with different feed such as seaweed, which would make cattle produce less gas. Maybe we just have to cut down the number of cows, but we can only do that if all of us eat less meat and dairy produce (cheese, butter, milk etc.). We can go some way towards achieving that if we avoid eating meat for one day a week. Imagine if all 66 million people in the UK only ever ate vegetables. That would have the same effect on CO_2 emissions as taking 2 million cars off the road.

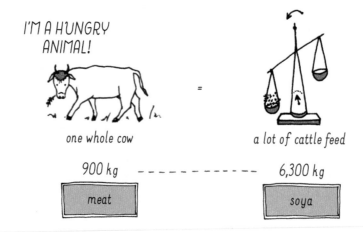

I'M A HUNGRY ANIMAL!

one whole cow

a lot of cattle feed

900 kg — — — — — — — — — — 6,300 kg

meat

soya

52 COWS EAT TOO MUCH

Cows, and of course other livestock, need to eat – a lot. They eat grass but they also get extra feed, often soya meal. Seven kilograms of soya are needed for every kilogram of beef. Work out how much that is for a 900-kilogram cow! Two-thirds of all agricultural land on our planet is used as grazing land or to grow cattle feed.

If you laid all the fields where soya is grown side by side, they would cover about 100 million hectares, an area as big as Germany, France, Belgium and the Netherlands put together. That's quite a lot! Soya for cattle feed is mostly grown in South America. Precious forests are cut down or pastures are turned into **soya plantations**. The Cerrado in Brazil is a magnificent savannah, home to animals like jaguars, giant anteaters and wolves. More and more of that natural environment is being destroyed to grow soya. Every year in the Amazon 600,000 hectares of forest are cut down and burned to grow soya.

With fewer forests, animal habitats are lost and less carbon dioxide is absorbed from the air. And more greenhouse gases in the atmosphere lead to rising temperatures. Another good reason to cut down on eating meat and dairy products.

53 COWS PRODUCE TOO MANY COWPATS

Every so often cows – and of course other livestock too – need to do their business. Farmers use some of the enormous piles of manure to fertilize the land. But there are too many cattle, so there is much too much **manure**. It contains unhealthy substances like **phosphates**, **nitrates** and **ammonia**. These can end up in the groundwater and make it acidic. Because of this pollution, the water needs extra purification before we can drink it. Also, more algae grow in the water, so it contains less oxygen and that's not good for the fish either.

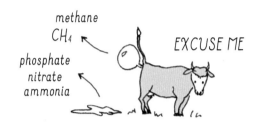

When there is too much manure, some plants, such as stinging nettles and brambles, grow a lot faster than they should. They begin to crowd out other plants, which will eventually disappear.

Luckily, things are going in the right direction in some places. Animal sheds are built in such a way that fewer pollutants escape. Manure is injected into the ground instead of being spread across the land. Obviously the best solution is still to produce less manure. That means fewer cattle. If all of us eat less meat, we will solve the problem of too many cowpats.

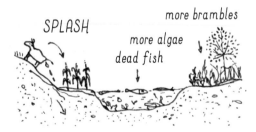

manure goes into groundwater and streams

BONUS FACT

Did you know that soon you might no longer need to kill an animal to eat real meat? Stem cells from the muscles of cows, chickens and other livestock are being used to 'grow' meat in laboratories. You can make 10,000 kilograms of meat from one stem cell! This should enormously reduce the number of cows, pigs, chickens and sheep. It's still extremely expensive to produce an artificial hamburger – over £200,000 – but this might change when it's done on a much larger scale.

54 TROPICAL FORESTS ARE BEING CHOPPED DOWN FOR CHOCOLATE

Indonesia is made up of more than 14,500 large and small islands. An enormous **tropical rainforest** grows there, with a huge number of different plants and trees. The forest is home to thousands of animal species. Sadly, there is a problem. Four-fifths, or 80%, of the original rainforest has been chopped down or burned to make room for agriculture. This is an area of 260,000 square kilometres, bigger than the United Kingdom. When it is cut down or burned it releases enormous quantities of greenhouse gases.

The rainforest has been replaced by oil palms, thousands and thousands of identical trees in neat rows. The **palm oil** extracted from their fruit is used in all kinds of food (including chocolate, soup, pizza and biscuits), as well as cleaning products, cosmetics and biofuels. Most of these products are eaten or used in rich countries.

So you're probably thinking, but oil palms are trees too? Yes, but they're not the same as tropical rainforest. For a start, they absorb much less carbon dioxide. Besides that, they don't provide a habitat or food for the animals that live there. Elephants, orangutans, tigers and rhinos have nowhere to go and they are dying out. A female orangutan takes ten years to become an adult, a male takes fifteen years. Mothers teach their young where to find the trees with the tastiest fruit. It takes a while before the youngsters can remember all of those places. If the trees disappear, the orangutans don't know what to do.

forest giants

canopy

bushes

forest floor

before

now

tropical rainforest growth

Orangutans are now one of the world's most endangered species, not just because their habitat is disappearing, but also because they are hunted for their meat. Only 800 Tapanuli orangutans, which live in the tropical rainforest of Sumatra, are left now. Did you know that you can do something about this? Whenever you're about to buy something, read the label. Does the list of ingredients include palm oil? If so, see if there's another product that doesn't contain it.

55 TREE RINGS CAN TELL US ABOUT CLIMATE CHANGE

You've probably seen trees that have been sawn through and you know they have rings in their trunks. If you count them, you can tell immediately how old the tree was. It works for trees that fell millions of years ago and have become fossilized as well as for trees that have been neatly sawn through.

You can see from the **tree rings** what the summer was like. A tree grows more in a warm wet summer than in a dry summer. That means the rings are thicker, which gave researcher **Michael Mann** an idea. He studied the rings in thousands of trees and measured how thick they were.

With that information he was able to draw a graph showing the average temperature on earth over a very long period. Between 1000 and 1900 it did not change all that much. But at the end of that line something unusual happened. Between 1800 and 1900 the line suddenly went up quite steeply. That is because the temperature rose very quickly from then on.

In the next few years, other researchers repeated the measurements. Michael Mann was right. In the last century in particular, the earth warmed up far more quickly than ever before. We know this because the trees told us!

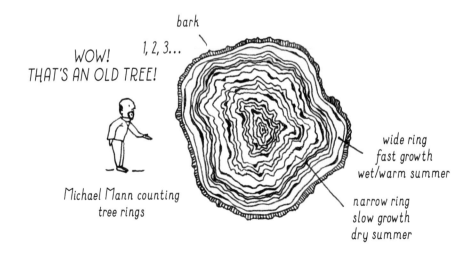

WOW!
THAT'S AN OLD TREE!

1, 2, 3...

bark

Michael Mann counting tree rings

wide ring
fast growth
wet/warm summer

narrow ring
slow growth
dry summer

4

THE EARTH IS GETTING MORE POLLUTED

56 LOOK OUT! DON'T BREATHE!

Imagine if you turned on the TV and the newsreader said it's dangerous to breathe. What are you going to do? Humans and other animals have to breathe in order to live. Ideally in clean, unpolluted air. Sadly, the air is not equally clean everywhere. You might live close to a busy road, where cars, lorries and motorbikes emit a lot of **soot** and **nitrogen dioxide**. There might be a factory nearby that emits dangerous substances. There might be a lot of fires burning in the area.

Particulates are tiny particles that float in the air. They are invisible to the naked eye. About 90% of them are natural. Over the oceans, they are mostly salt and sand particles. The rest are caused by human beings. As well as particulates, we also breathe in soot, ozone and nitrogen dioxide. None of these is good for our bodies. They cause us problems with our airways, giving us asthma and bronchitis for instance.

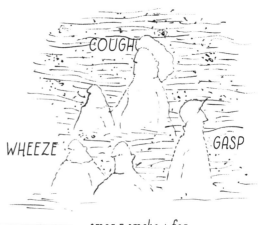

smog = smoke + fog

Sometimes the air pollution is so bad that smog is formed. The word smog, meaning a mixture of smoke and fog, originated in England. Smog was discovered in the 19th century when a lot of coal was burned, giving off smoke that hung in the air in foggy weather. Now it means air pollution you can see. Sunlight turns the pollutants emitted by traffic and factories into ozone. That gas protects us against harmful UV rays high in the atmosphere, but it is not good for us if it is close to the earth. Then it literally hangs as a yellowish brown cloud making it difficult to breathe. If there is a **fog warning** on the weather forecast, it's better not to go running or play outdoor sports.

BONUS FACT

22 September is World Car-Free Day, when many cities all over the world ban cars. Some cities even hold several car-free days every year, to show residents how nice a city without cars can be. You can safely walk, cycle or ride your scooter down the middle of the road and there is a lot less air pollution.

atmospheric brown cloud

WHERE AM I?

3,000 metres

57 IN SOME PLACES, IT GETS DARK IN THE MIDDLE OF THE DAY

In Chinese cities like Beijing and Shanghai and in New Delhi in India there is sometimes a quarter less light than usual. That is due to the **Asian** or **Atmospheric Brown Cloud**, a massive cloud that hangs over large areas of China and India from November to May. It was first seen in satellite photos in the 1990s. Now the cloud is hanging for longer and longer. According to scientists it's at least 3,000 metres thick. It's formed by soot particles from wood fires, pollution from cars and lorries and factory emissions. The dirty brown cloud is very unhealthy for people who breathe it in every day. Scientists estimate that it kills about 2 million people every year.

The cloud also affects the climate. It hangs over the Himalayas, the highest mountain range in the world. There is so much snow and ice there that they are sometimes called Asia's water towers. Large quantities of fresh water flow into rivers from Himalayan glaciers and snowfields. Billions of people depend on it. But climate change, partly due to the brown cloud, makes the ice and snow melt more quickly. Sometimes the snow melts so quickly that it forms lakes. When they suddenly empty they can sweep whole villages away. Over time the glaciers are also getting smaller, so there is less meltwater and therefore less fresh water.

So it's important to get rid of the brown cloud as quickly as possible. Then people will be able to breathe safely again and have enough fresh water to drink.

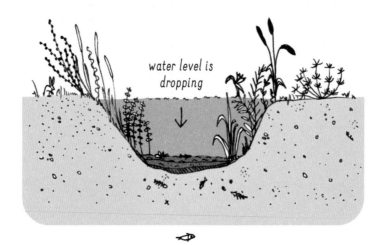

water level is dropping

58 FRESH WATER IS DRYING UP

Wetlands or **marshland** are a very important part of the water cycle. These are areas with plenty of fresh water, usually between the land and the sea or ocean. They are often home to various species of animals and many kinds of plants grow there, so they are really important for biodiversity. When there is heavy rain, the marshy areas absorb the surplus water and they are a storage tank for fresh water. Wetlands can be found all over the world. The Pantanal in South America is one example; some islands in Oceania are largely marshland and so is Hudson Bay in Canada. There are also wetlands in the lowlands of northern Europe, for instance in the Netherlands and the Flanders region of Belgium.

Unfortunately, we haven't taken good care of those water supplies. Often, too much water is used from the marshy areas and that causes problems. In Spain, for instance, large wetlands have been destroyed in order to grow pineapples, mandarins, almonds and grapes. The mouth of the Yellow River in China is dry for nearly 200 days a year because farmers pump up too much water to irrigate their cotton fields. Sadly, a lot of fish species have already disappeared from the Yellow River. If we want wetlands and all the creatures that live there to survive we need to treat them with much more care.

59 WAITER! THERE'S ~~A FLY~~ PLASTIC IN MY SOUP

OBSTACLE AHEAD!
plastic in the soup

Charles Moore

Look around you. Chances are you can see something that's made of **plastic**. It might be a plastic wrapper with biscuits in it, a cup you drink out of or even the chair you're sitting on. Plastic is actually another name for synthetic material. Bakelite was the first synthetic material. It was invented by a Belgian called **Leo Baekeland** in 1907 and it quickly took over the world. About 311 billion kilograms of plastic are produced every year, and the quantity is still rising.

Plastic is great. You can do all kinds of things with it. But there is one big drawback: you can't get rid of it. Larger plastic breaks down into smaller pieces over time, but that's all. It is not biodegradable. Every year about 5 million tons of plastic waste end up in the seas and oceans. That's equal to about a full lorry load every minute! It is mainly from litter – plastic bottles, sweet wrappings, plastic bags – that we throw away in the street. It blows into the rivers and then it's carried down to the sea.

In 1997, to his surprise, Captain Charles Moore found a huge amount of plastic in the middle of the Pacific. He called it **plastic soup**. We now know that there are five enormous sinkholes, or **gyres**, in the oceans. These massive whirlpools are caused by currents. All the waste is drawn towards them. There is more plastic in the sea in those five places than anywhere else.

Besides that, there are plastic **hotspots** at which there is a lot more plastic in the sea than usual. The Mediterranean is one. The rivers that flow into it carry plastic. It is held back by the narrow Strait of Gibraltar, which acts as a kind of bottleneck. Other hotspots are on bays with large coastal towns, on water where there is a lot of industry nearby or at places where rivers flow into the sea.

More and more people are trying to do something about the plastic soup. For instance **Boyan Slat**, a young Dutch inventor, was shocked at the plastic polluting the water when he was on a diving holiday in Greece. The device he built to clear plastic waste floating in the sea has been in use since 2018. You can find out more about his project at www.theoceancleanup.com.

UNLOAD!

HERE GOES!

plastic

1 lorry per minute
5 million tons per year

60 160,000 PLASTIC BAGS PER SECOND!

Do you take a reusable bag to the shops with you? Or do you ask for a **plastic bag** each time? Did you know that every second 160,000 plastic bags are given out all over the world. By the time you've read this sentence again there will be another half a million bags in circulation. That's just under 10 million bags per minute, half a billion in an hour and 13 billion in a 24-hour day. Barely 1 to 3% of all those bags are recycled. Huge numbers of them end up in the oceans, where they form plastic soup with the other waste.

Among the creatures swimming in the sea are sea turtles. They can't tell the difference between a jellyfish and a plastic bag. They just see the thing floating in front of them as a tasty bite to eat. They eat the bag and that causes problems. Plastic cannot be digested, so it stays in their stomachs and intestines, and they can't excrete it. They could have a long life ahead of them (sea turtles live to be 80 years old), but the plastic in their stomachs kills them. The same thing happens with whales. They have kilograms of plastic in their stomachs. That stops them eating, and so they starve. Albatrosses can't tell the difference between a nice fish and a coloured piece of plastic. They eat it or feed it to their chicks. You can guess what happens, right? Nearly 400 animal species are endangered because they eat plastic or get entangled in it. If they don't die from the plastic on them, they are quite likely to be poisoned. Plastic contains all kinds of toxic substances that are released into the water.

there's confusion at sea

Most of the plastic that ends up in the sea is the single-use kind: soft-drink bottles, biscuit packaging, salad boxes. You can help to reduce the plastic soup yourself by buying as few prepacked products as possible. Try asking your parents to shop where everything is sold in bulk without packaging. You just take boxes or bags with you. If some things are still packaged, recycle all plastic bottles, tins and drinks cartons and *never* throw litter in the street.

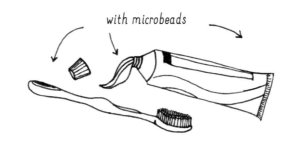

with microbeads

61 YOUR TOOTHPASTE AND YOUR SHAMPOO CONTAIN PLASTIC

You might not believe it, but it's true: toothpaste, shampoo, cosmetics, sunscreen and all kinds of toiletries and household products can contain **microbeads**, which are tiny balls or fragments of plastic. They make your toothpaste more abrasive, or make it easier to remove dead skin cells with a body scrub.

These very small pieces of plastic usually end up in the sink. They're washed away and go into the drains. The water filter system is not designed to remove such small particles, so masses of them end up in the plastic soup in rivers, oceans and seas. The minute fragments are swallowed by marine creatures and make them ill.

A number of countries, including the United States, Canada, Australia and Britain, have now banned microbeads in products. To find out if there are any in the things you buy, check to see if the ingredients include polypropylene (PP) or polyethylene (PE). If there is a triangle on them with a '0' in it (the Zero Plastic Inside logo), that means there are no microbeads in them. Go to **www.beatthemicrobead.org** to see which products contain microbeads.

zero plastic inside

BONUS FACT

Instead of asking for wedding presents, Prince Harry and his wife Meghan asked their guests to donate to organizations that clear up plastic. A royal gesture, in our opinion!

There's more plastic on the beach than you think!

62 THERE'S PLASTIC IN YOUR SWIMMING COSTUME AND MAYBE IN YOUR SWEATER

Have a look at the label in your swimming costume, your sportswear or your fleece. If there's **nylon**, **acrylic**, **polyester** or another synthetic material in them, they also contain a kind of **plastic**. Often those kinds of clothes are even made from recycled plastic bottles. So you think, great, recycling is good. Yes, but there's a problem. When you put those clothes in the washing machine, lots of little microfibres literally come out in the wash. They go into the drainage system and from there all the way into the sea. A third of all microplastics in the ocean come from microfibres in our clothing. The tiny fibres are even spread through the air. They are found literally everywhere, even in places where there are no people. And they are in our food, in fish, mussels and other marine creatures and also in honey. So eventually we reabsorb the fibres. The older your clothes are, the more of these microfibres they shed.

Now people are trying very hard to find solutions. For instance, they are working on special wash bags that trap the fibres during washing. Washing machine designers are seeing whether they can make better filters that stop the fibres going through. You can do something yourself by avoiding wearing synthetic clothes as much as you can. Choose natural fibres like cotton, linen, wool and silk. Try to wash your synthetic clothes as little as possible. The material will wear better and not lose as many fibres. Your clothes will last longer and you will also save on water, energy and detergent.

It's 100% natural!

63 BIODEGRADABLE ... BUT NOT IN A FISH'S STOMACH

biodegradable plastic

Some plastic packaging has a leaf logo on it. That means the plastic is **biodegradable** and after a time it disappears. But don't be too quick to shout hooray. It might take up to two years for this type of plastic to disappear on your own compost heap in your back garden. Biodegradable actually means that it disappears completely in seven weeks if it is put into a special machine and heated to 65°C. It stays a lot longer in the stomach of a fish or sea turtle – too long for the poor animal to survive.

Does the packaging say **bioplastic?** Those are plastics made from natural products like sugar cane or starch. Not all bioplastic is biodegradable. Sometimes it stays just as long in the sea as normal plastic. So never just throw plastic away in the street. In the end it always comes back to you. It's much better to use as little plastic as possible.

fresh fish with salad and chips

64 PLASTIC AT THE BOTTOM OF THE OCEAN

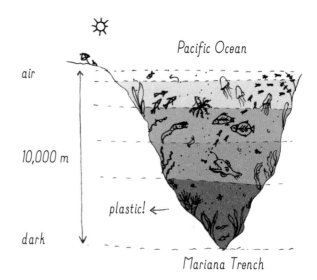

Have you ever heard of the Mariana Trench in the Pacific Ocean? It's the deepest place on earth; at its lowest point it's over 10,000 metres deep. It's very cold and dark, so not exactly a cheerful place. But even at those depths, unusual sea creatures can live. There are amphipods, which are similar to small prawns, and strange fish that have almost transparent skin. And sure enough, there is plastic floating around. A plastic bag was actually found on the ocean bed in the Mariana Trench. Most of the plastic was floating six kilometres deep, about 335 pieces per square kilometre. It was mainly single-use plastic such as packaging, plastic bags and bottles.

Scientists are very concerned about this. There are cracks in the earth layer at the bottom of the trench, from which cold and hot springs bubble up. They release minerals into the water. The minerals are food for bacteria, which in turn feed corals, worms, fish and sea anemones. All the amphipods in the Mariana Trench had microplastics in their bodies. These were mostly microfibres from synthetic clothing, but sometimes they were **microbeads**. If life so deep in the ocean is already affected, that's really bad news. It means that ecosystems are polluted right into the depths of the ocean.

BONUS FACT

Scientists have also found microplastics in the ice around Spitsbergen and Canada. They must have come from the air. According to the scientists, that means that people are probably breathing in plastic all the time. A horrifying thought!

65 CIGARETTES ARE BAD FOR YOU

As you're so smart you know of course that it's better not to start smoking. It's very bad for your health. But did you know that **cigarette ends** are also really bad for the environment? Every year about 4.5 billion cigarette ends end up in nature worldwide. That's a very big part of all the rubbish you see on land and in the sea. They pollute the earth and the oceans. The filters in cigarette ends only degrade very slowly in nature. It takes at least two years for a cigarette filter to break down completely. And even then minute fibres are left, which do not break down completely but end up in the water or the ground. When cigarette ends go into the water they are often eaten by fish. The nicotine that is still in them and the synthetic material in the filters makes the fish ill.

Of course you don't smoke, but maybe you chew **gum**. Don't throw it away in the street! It takes at least 20 years for gum to break down completely. Not only is it dirty, it can also be dangerous for small animals. A little bird hopping around on the ground can get stuck in a blob of chewing gum. It can't fly away and it dies. Put your chewing gum and other rubbish in a rubbish bin, then it can be disposed of properly.

LAST BREATH   COUGH

smoking kills

66 CALL IN THE ARMY, THE PLASTIC ENEMY IS COMING

Close your eyes and imagine a long, winding river. The water is flowing along beautifully. Now imagine the river is full of plastic bottles, bags, sweet wrappers, empty crisp packets and other rubbish, so you can't even see the water any more. It's literally a river of plastic rubbish. It's already looking a bit less delightful! But it's actually happening. In **Bandung**, a big city in Indonesia, there is so much rubbish in the river that the water has stopped flowing. Everything has literally come to a standstill. Food in cities like Bandung used to be packed in banana leaves. Now it's packed in plastic. Besides that, a lot of people have flocked into the city. They just throw their rubbish into the river, which causes a terrible mess. It's so bad that the government has sent in the army to try to clear the river of rubbish and get it flowing again. But really it's a hopeless task. The soldiers fish enormous amounts of plastic out of the water, but every day just as much is put back. Plastic is the biggest enemy for the **Indonesian army** at the moment. Now the government is trying to persuade people not to throw any more plastic into the river. It even gives people a small payment if they recycle the plastic. But it will be a long time before all the plastic is cleared away and the rivers can flow freely again. Luckily, governments are more and more aware of the problem and are trying to do something about it. On the island of **Bali** in Indonesia single-use plastic has been banned since June 2019. Anyone using it gets a stiff fine. The aim is eventually to reduce the amount of plastic waste by 70%.

UH-OH

plastic monster

67 NEARLY ALL PLASTIC COMES FROM TEN RIVERS

Of course we all want less plastic to end up in the sea. Scientists are looking for ways to make the sea **plastic-free** again. It obviously makes more sense if we all use less plastic or if we can at least stop the plastic before it ends up in the ocean.

Nearly all the plastic in our oceans comes from ten rivers: the Blue River, the Indus, the Yellow River, the Hai, the Nile, the Ganges, the Pearl River, the Amur, the Niger and the Mekong. Nearly all of them are in Asia and Africa. They are big rivers that flow through places where millions of people live, cities in poorer countries where rubbish is often not collected. There are also no recycling schemes for plastic.

The good news is that if we can remove the plastic from those rivers before they reach the sea, we can solve a very big problem. But we're not quite there yet.

BONUS FACT

The **Big Jump** is an event held in Europe every year. Thousands of people in different cities around the world jump into the water in big rivers. This draws attention to pollution in the hope that governments will do more to clean up rivers and streams and keep them clean. Would you like to join in? The Big Jump takes place on the second Sunday in July. Find out online where you can jump.

rubbish flows out of rivers into the sea

WHAT A LOT OF NONSENSE!

makes you strong   brings you luck   keeps you fit

68 POACHERS MOSTLY HUNT THREATENED SPECIES

Poachers are people who hunt animals without a licence. It makes no difference to them that there are very few of some of these animals left. In fact, poachers specifically go after **endangered species** because those are the ones they can make the most money from. Every year, the trade in endangered species brings in between about 7 and 15 billion pounds. That's a huge amount of money. After the loss of their habitats, it is the second biggest reason why these poor animals are facing extinction.

Elephants are poachers' main victims. Every year 30,000 elephants are killed for their ivory. The ivory trade is banned but poachers don't care about that. All kinds of artefacts are made from the tusks. If the poachers can't be stopped there will be no more wild elephants in 30 years' time.

Rhinos are hunted for their horns. In 2007 poachers killed as many as 1,028 rhinos in South Africa. That's an average of three a day. And all

because some people believe that powdered rhino horn makes them stronger or fitter. At this rate they can be expected to disappear even more quickly than elephants.

Wild tigers are almost extinct in Asia. There are only 3,900 left. They are hunted in order to make 'tiger wine'. The tiger's carcass is suspended in a vat of rice wine for a long time. The stuff that is brewed is supposed to make you 'as strong as a tiger'. Of course that's nonsense.

Some rich people enjoy hunting animals themselves. They can pay thousands of pounds to shoot an elephant, a tiger or a rhino, which they then hang on the wall at home as a trophy. A weird hobby, in our opinion.

Luckily, there are organizations that are trying to stop poachers and other hunters. The trade in endangered species is banned everywhere in the world.

I think we caught a mermaid by mistake!

69 WE ARE TAKING TOO MANY FISH FROM THE SEA

People often say, there are plenty more fish in the sea. Well, that used to be true. But three billion people, slightly less than half the world's population, need **fish** to survive. It's their main source of animal food. For millions of people, fishing is also their main income. For a long time we didn't think the seas and oceans would run out of fish. Now, scientists think differently.

Since 1950 more fish have been taken from the sea than go into it. Fish just can't just reproduce fast enough. Some methods wipe out fish stocks even faster. Nets several miles long catch massive quantities of fish from certain parts of the sea. If that is done too often, the fish don't have time to grow to adulthood and they die out.

There are also a lot of **by-catches** with those large nets – fish, turtles and even seabirds that are unlucky enough to get caught in the nets and fished up. They die and are often just thrown back into the sea. No one cares about them.

Trawler nets are dragged across the seabed, damaging coral, plants and mussel and oyster beds. In Africa and Asia, fishermen pack dynamite into empty soft drink cans. They set it off close to a reef. The dead fish come to the surface, but of course the reef is permanently damaged. In Asia they use **cyanide**. Fishermen spray the poison into the cracks in the reef where it stuns the fish. They can then be caught easily, but it also affects other sea creatures and the coral and they die.

If we want to have fish in our seas and oceans in the future, we need to think carefully about how we fish. Because, let's face it, an ocean with no life in it is a pretty depressing thought.

70 WE THROW AWAY LORRY LOADS OF FOOD

Imagine five big buckets full of unwanted food. Sounds horrible, right? But that's about the quantity each of us throws away every year. It's mostly bread, dairy products, vegetables, potatoes and fruit that end up in the bin. Apparently sweets and biscuits are usually eaten up! If you add together all the food we throw away, it fills thousands of lorries. And added to that are the 60 litres of soft drinks, juice, wine, beer, coffee and tea that each of us pours down the sink every year.

Worldwide, about **one third** of all the food produced is turned into rubbish. In developing countries a lot is lost during harvests or when the food is processed. In rich countries the food mostly ends up in the bin in homes or shops.

> ## BONUS FACT
>
> We need fossil fuels to produce food. That means you need two litres of petrol a day for all your food. Petrol is a fossil fuel, so the food you waste also creates more carbon dioxide emissions.

Of course that is a huge **waste,** especially when you think that a billion people in the world don't have enough to eat. But what is more, producing all that food and drink uses a lot of energy. And all of it has to be packed and transported. Nearly a

third of greenhouse gas emissions comes from food production. If we then just throw it away, that is obviously even more of a shame. All that food was produced by people and it's crazy that someone should have to work so hard for something that eventually ends up in the bin.

SQUASH IT DOWN!

X 5

food thrown away per person each year

5

EFFECTS OF A HOTTER AND MORE POLLUTED PLANET

WE'LL HAVE A NEW EARTH, PLEASE

HAS EVERYTHING RUN OUT?

at the checkout

71 ONE PLANET IS NOT ENOUGH FOR US

Since the 1970s, humans have consumed more per year than the earth can produce in one year. We take more fish from the oceans and rivers than can be replaced in one year. We chop down more trees than can grow in one year. We replace more nature with concrete and agricultural land than the earth can cope with. We emit more carbon dioxide and other greenhouse gases than the forests and oceans can absorb. The Global Footprint Network has calculated the day on which people will have used up all the raw materials and food the earth can produce in one year. Added to them is the waste the earth can process in one year. That is called **Earth Overshoot Day** or **Ecological Debt Day**, the day on which everything runs out.

In 1990 the day was 6 November. Ten years later it went forward to 9 October. In 2019 the date was 29 July. So every year we live 'on credit' for five months. In those months, we use up the earth's remaining stocks and cause more pollution than can be cleared up. We really have to make sure the day goes back to later in the year again.

72 WE'LL SOON HAVE WET FEET

We'd like you to do a little experiment. Put a piece of ice into a glass of water and mark where the water comes up to. Then, let the ice melt completely. Measure the water level again. What do you see? The water level has hardly changed.

In Fact 15 we said that the **North Pole** is made up completely of sea ice. There is no land underneath. The ice floats on the ocean. When the ice melts, nothing happens. The seawater level will not go up or down.

But it's not the same with the land ice in **Greenland** in the north and **Antarctica** in the south. There is a very thick ice cap on Greenland, with lots of glaciers. If that ice melts, the level of the oceans goes up all over the world by as much as 70 metres. As long as the ice only melts on the edges of Greenland there's no real danger. But if the ice in the centre of Greenland starts to melt then things don't look too good. The meltwater would then look for a way down, carrying large blocks of ice or glaciers along with it. These would end up in the oceans, where they would melt much more quickly. The land ice in Antarctica and the glaciers in the high mountains can also cause the sea level to rise.

In the summer of 2017 an enormous iceberg broke off from Antarctica. It was so big it could have bridged the gap between the European mainland and Britain, so there wouldn't be a need for the Channel Tunnel. Because it was an iceberg on the edge of Antarctica that was floating on water, it probably didn't make much difference to the water level. But if the glaciers in Antarctica melt, we will soon get our feet wet.

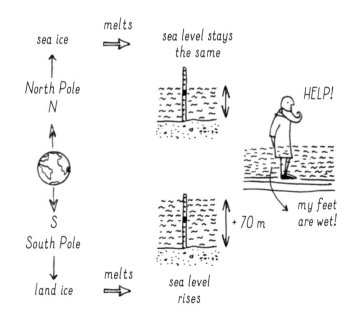

coral under stress in warm water

73 YOU'LL SOON BE ABLE TO TAKE A WARM BATH IN THE OCEAN
(AND THAT ISN'T AS GREAT AS IT SOUNDS)

Water is pretty amazing and it has a will of its own. Fill a bowl with water and put it in the freezer. When you get it out again, the water seems to have got 'bigger'. It projects above the rim of the bowl. The same thing happens when you boil water. Water is 'smallest' or takes up the least room at 4°C. So rising sea levels are caused not just by land ice melting but also by water spreading into the oceans as it gets warmer. Whenever the ocean water warms up a degree, sea level rises one metre. The air is up to 1°C warmer than in 1850–1900. Luckily, water warms up more slowly. At the moment the sea level is 20 centimetres higher than it was in 1850.

When ocean water warms up, that also has serious consequences for marine life. Warmth is not good for fish and other sea creatures. In Fact 23 we explained how important coral reefs are. They feed on the algae that live on them and give them their colour. But if the seawater warms up by just 2°C, the coral becomes stressed. Then it expels the algae and they have nothing to eat. The corals lose their colour and are **bleached**. After a while they die off completely.

In 2016–2017, a thousand kilometres of the **Great Barrier Reef** in Australia, the biggest coral reef in the world, disappeared in exactly that way. Not only was the coral killed off but all the fish and other marine creatures that lived there left or died. All that was left was an empty ocean. We now know that half of all the coral in the world has already gone. If the sea temperature rises by 2°C, that would be a disaster for the whole ocean as an ecosystem.

74 THINGS ARE GETTING DIFFICULT IF YOU LIVE NEAR WATER

The ocean level is rising. That's very bad news for people who live near the coast. Bangladesh is a densely populated country in Asia. Scientists predict that 17% of it will be under water by 2050. Millions of people will have to move. There's a reason why Belgium and the Netherlands are called the Low Countries. If the **seawater level** rises, higher embankments, called dikes, will need to be built, to try to keep the water back.

It will be difficult for cities near the coast. These are often big cities like Miami, New York, Boston and New Orleans in the United States, Mumbai in India, Osaka and Nagoya in Japan and Guangzhou and Shenzhen in China. They will have to cope with serious floods.

It's even worse if you live on an **island** in the middle of the ocean. Five tiny islands in the Solomon Islands, a group of hundreds of islands in the Pacific, have already disappeared as the ocean level rises. Each was only as big as between one and five football pitches, but parts of larger islands are also disappearing under water. Whole villages are being wiped off the map. For instance, there were 25 families living on Nuatambu. Eleven houses have disappeared into the sea. Half the inhabitants have moved to a higher island nearby. Scientists are afraid the same thing could happen with the Maldives in the Indian Ocean and the Marshall Islands in the Pacific. The people living there will have to move.

In rich countries, a lot of work is now going on to keep the rising water back. But for poorer countries it's a lot harder. For millions of people, life there will become very difficult if the sea level rises.

ISLAND? WHAT ISLAND?

the sunken Solomon Islands

algae and coral are dying in the depths of the sea

75 NO ONE IS HAPPY ABOUT ACIDIFICATION

The water in our vast oceans absorbs a lot of **carbon dioxide** from the atmosphere. In the last 200 years it amounts to at least 500 billion tons. Scientists use the pH scale to measure the acidity of substances. The enormous quantity of carbon dioxide lowers the pH in the oceans, which means that the oceans become more acidic. It's like fizzy water and still water. Fizzy water has more carbon in it and so it's more 'acidic' than still water. Just try drinking a glass of still and a glass of fizzy water and you'll see the difference straight away.

Since the mid-19th century the water in the ocean has gone down by a pH factor of 0.1. That doesn't sound like much, but it has serious consequences. **Acidification** attacks lime, just as vinegar can remove limescale from taps. That is bad for the shells of oysters, mussels and other shellfish. Their shells become thinner and they are more easily eaten up by predators. They also become more susceptible to all kinds of diseases. Sometimes all the young die because their shells don't grow fast enough.

Another problem is that algae don't grow as well because of the higher acid levels. Coral needs the algae to feed on. If they disappear then the coral reefs will disappear too. Furthermore, the higher acid level attacks the coral's skeleton. The coral reefs are not as strong and suffer more from pollution and storms. So we need to do everything we can to stop the ocean becoming more acidic.

76 WHAT IF THE FREEZER ACTUALLY BREAKS DOWN?

Yes, you read that correctly – the earth has an actual freezer, and it's called **permafrost**. It's a layer that is permanently frozen. About a fifth of all the land on earth consists of permafrost. Those regions are mostly in Canada, Alaska, Siberia and Scandinavia. In summer, the top part of the layer (the **active layer**) melts or thaws. Then, in winter everything freezes again.

As the earth warms up, larger and larger areas of permafrost are thawing. The whole layer is becoming smaller and thinner. That is dangerous. If you unplug a freezer and leave it for a couple of days, after a while it will start to smell bad because the food is going off. The same happens with permafrost. The layer contains all kinds of plant and animal remains. If they thaw out, bacteria can get in and break down the material, releasing large amounts of carbon dioxide and methane. Climatologists are very worried about that. If the extra greenhouse gases get into the atmosphere they might make the earth warm up even faster. So we mustn't let the temperature of our freezer drop any further. Otherwise we might reach a **tipping point** (see Fact 96). That's the point at which a very big change happens in a short time. Then we will no longer be able to reverse the effects.

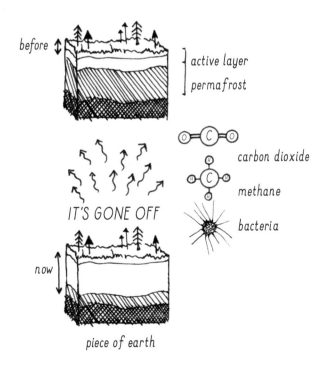

before

active layer
permafrost

carbon dioxide

methane

bacteria

IT'S GONE OFF

now

piece of earth

HURRICANE

1. sun warms the oceans
2. water evaporates, low pressure area develops
3. air is sucked in
4. hot air is pushed upwards, pressure rises
5. air is pressed down, eye is formed (E)
6. spirals develop high in the air

77 WIND, STORMS, HURRICAAAANES!

As temperatures on the earth rise, the weather is becoming more extreme. That means, for instance, that a period of drought lasts longer. Without water, fruit is smaller, grain does not grow as well and the whole harvest can fail. There are also more **heatwaves**, periods that are much hotter than normal and all you can do is lie in a swimming pool to cool off. During heatwaves **forest fires** can break out. In 2018, for instance, that happened not just in California but also in Sweden, a country in the far north where summers are not usually that hot. There were even fires in the Siberian taiga. At least 10 million hectares of forest were destroyed. Nearly 200 people died in Japan in the summer of 2018 in the worst floods the country had ever seen.

You've probably heard about violent hurricanes with names like Mitch, Katrina, Wilma and Haiyan, which have claimed many victims in the past few years and caused a lot of damage. Of course, there have always been natural disasters such as **floods, hurricanes, tornadoes** and **storms**. Not counting a disease like the plague, the worst natural disaster was in 1931, when a million people died in flooding in China. Now scientists have all kinds of state-of-the-art electronic devices to help them forecast the weather. So people can evacuate an area when a storm or hurricane is on its way and fewer people die. Even so there is three times as much extreme weather as in 1980. Many scientists put that down to global warming.

78 IT'S GETTING HOT IN THE CITY

Have you ever been in a city on a warm summer's day, or maybe you live in a city? Then you might have noticed that it was much hotter there than in the countryside or on the coast.

There are a few reasons for this. First of all it's because of the city's **albedo** (see Fact 32). There's a lot of black asphalt, the buildings are quite dark and often you see squares without any grass or trees. All those dark objects absorb the sun's rays and give off a lot of heat. They make the temperature rise.

The wind cannot blow as much between the buildings in the city, so the city cools down less than the countryside. Also, there is a lot of traffic and a lot more energy is used, for air conditioning or in factories for example. That sometimes makes cities up to 8°C hotter than the countryside. So when it is a pleasant 23°C in the forest, the temperature in the city can go up to as much as 31°C. The city becomes a **heat island**.

By 2050, 68% of people will live in cities. We have to make sure that all those cities remain habitable. They need more greenery and less traffic. Above all, it must be enjoyable to walk and cycle and to eat an ice cream, without it melting immediately of course!

Some people are now trying to make cities greener. They are secretly planting seeds and bulbs in the ground, which grow up between the stones. That's called **guerrilla gardening**. For instance you can plant narcissus or tulip bulbs somewhere. No one sees, but in the spring they produce beautiful flowers that attract bees and other insects. Sunflower seeds and pumpkin seeds are even easier to plant. Poppies and marigolds are colourful and herbs like mint make the city smell nice. What are you waiting for? Get gardening!

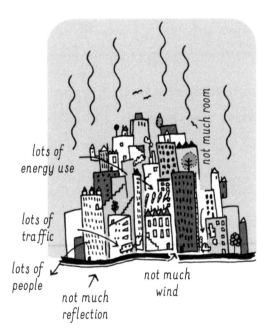

lots of energy use

not much room

lots of traffic

lots of people

not much reflection

not much wind

Welcome to the simmering city

79 FOREST FIRES

You may have seen the television images of the big **forest fires** that broke out everywhere in the summer of 2018 and 2019. In the Greek capital, Athens, they killed 91 people, more than any other forest fire since 1900. In Portugal and Spain large areas of forest went up in flames in 2017. And in the United States the fire brigade struggled to put out a vast area of California. Many Hollywood stars lost their homes. The village of Paradise in Northern California might once have been a real paradise, but the flames wiped it off the map.

A fire needs three things: flammable material, a spark to set it alight and oxygen to keep it burning. There were plenty of those things in the European forest fires in particular. After a wet winter there was plenty of greenery. That was followed by a heatwave, with high temperatures and no rain. The greenery dried out. All it took was a small spark to start a blaze. That sometimes happened because people were careless or started fires deliberately. But more often the forest fires were caused by **lightning strikes**. With climate change we get more thunderstorms and so more flashes of lightning that can set everything ablaze.

Climatologists predict that in the future we will have twice as many heatwaves as we do now. Combined with more lightning strikes that means more forest fires. The annual number of **bushfires** in Australia trebled in 2019, gaining worldwide attention as more than 18,000,000 hectares of land burned. So the future doesn't look bright for our forests and everything that lives in them.

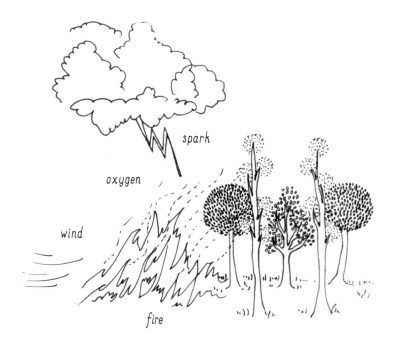

spark

oxygen

wind

fire

COLD, ME?
NOT AT ALL!

I'm ready for winter

80 A WARMER CLIMATE BUT FREEZING COLD WINTERS

Here's a really big question. How come we get freezing cold winters when the climate is warming up? There was plenty of snow on the mountains this year, which was good for skiing. Some days it was so cold you had to wear two layers of clothing. Here's the answer. First of all, remember there is a big difference between climate and weather. Climate covers a long period, maybe 15 or 30 years, and an average is taken. We know the average temperature is rising. Weather is local and temporary. It can also change suddenly. You're in your swimming costume ready to go and sunbathe, and suddenly it starts raining.

Secondly, it's quite possible that in some parts of the world climate change means **harder winters**. For instance it was very cold in large parts of the United States in January 2019.

That was due to a **polar vortex** high in the atmosphere. Cold air blew across the American continent from the North Pole. It was bitterly cold there, but in other parts of the world it was much warmer than usual. Scientists also believe that warmer temperatures at the North Pole lead to harder winters in the United States, even though the earth is generally warming up.

Sometimes global warming even causes heavy snow. The winter of 2006 was the first time Lake Erie in the north of the United States did not freeze right over. So the water in the lake was able to evaporate. The water fell from the clouds as snow. A huge amount of snow, in fact.

Anyhow, the climate is becoming much less predictable. And maybe that is exactly what worries scientists most.

81 MIGRATORY BIRDS ARE LOSING THEIR WAY

Migratory birds are having a difficult time. They have to fly to different areas in the world in order to survive. It gets too hot or too cold where they are and there is not enough food left. They leave and travel vast distances in search of a better place. **Swallows**, for instance, breed in northern Europe in the spring and summer. When it gets too cold they fly to warmer places in Asia, Africa and South America. Birds are smart. They know exactly where to go to find food. They usually choose a regular route and go to the same place.

Unfortunately, climate change is causing problems for birds. It's warmer on average, so spring starts a little earlier. When the migratory birds arrive, the caterpillars and larvae they usually feed on have already turned into butterflies or moths. So the birds can't find enough food for their young. Some years they die; those that survive are usually weaker and unable to manage the journey south.

Climate change also means more storms, hurricanes, floods, heatwaves and other extreme weather events. If migratory birds are caught up in them, they cannot get to their destination.

Satellites in the air and birdwatchers on the ground are monitoring the situation. Some satellites record weather data. Other equipment photographs the ground and observes the areas where there are birds. That information is gathered with observations by birdwatchers. Recent years have seen a fast decline in the number of migratory birds. Many look for other places to overwinter, but because of climate change a lot of migratory birds don't have that option any more.

BONUS FACT

People all over the world are trying to help migratory birds. European nature conservation groups are working with people in Africa. Together they are making sure that certain areas are reforested so that migratory birds have better places to spend the winter.

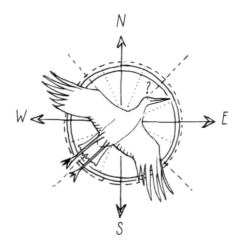

migratory birds are losing their bearings

COOCHY-COO

SWEET!

CHERISH THEM!

82 WHAT'S HAPPENING TO THE CREEPY-CRAWLIES?

Do you start screaming if a beetle walks across your arm? Or do you wave your arms about wildly if you see a wasp? A lot of people think we'd be better off without some **insects**. Unfortunately they don't realize that insects are necessary for life. We need them to pollinate our flowers and crops. They are food for birds, frogs, toads, salamanders, lizards and a whole lot of other creatures. They prevent pests attacking crops. They recycle food and manure, which keeps the soil healthy. Without insects, animal diversity would very quickly decline. The larger animals would disappear along with the insects.

Insects are the largest group of animals on earth. One million species have already been identified, but scientists think that a million might not have been studied yet. Sadly, their numbers are declining very fast. In some places there are up to 75% fewer insects than there used to be. At the moment bees, ants and beetles are dying out eight times faster than mammals, birds and reptiles.

If they continue to die out at that rate, there won't be any left by the end of the century.

But why are they disappearing? There are several reasons. Firstly, we use too many poisons or **pesticides** to protect our plants and crops. They wipe out all the insects and often a whole ecosystem. That is tragic, because there are enough ecologically safe ways to grow food without using pesticides. Secondly, built-up areas often leave insects nowhere to live. There is nowhere on streets or squares where they can build their nests. Not enough flowers grow for them to find food. Thirdly, insects can also get sick. A virus can wipe out a whole population. Because of climate change, some insects normally only found in Africa now also survive in Europe. Sometimes these exotic insects eat up the native species and change the whole ecosystem.

Next time, leave beetles and wasps alone as they go past. We need them very badly.

83 IT'S TOO HOT IN THE RAINFOREST

It may surprise you to learn that some insects are really bothered by heat, especially in the **tropical rainforest**. Normally insects, just like humans, adapt fairly quickly to change. But the climate is changing fast now, too fast for insects to keep up.

Scientists have been counting the number of insects in the **El Yunque** rainforest in Puerto Rico for many years. In 1976 there were 60 times as many insects as in 2013. There is no agriculture around El Yunque. No insecticides are used and there is no building. Researchers are almost certain that climate change is a factor. The average temperature has risen by two degrees in that period. Tropical insects are often very special. They adapt to their habitat in various ways. When there is a minor change, even a one degree difference in the temperature, their world is turned upside down. They can't get used to the new conditions quickly enough, and they soon die out.

When insects disappear the number of insect-eaters declines. For instance, fewer birds and lizards are found in El Yunque these days. So you can see that every link in the food chain is important. The disappearance of just one animal affects the whole forest.

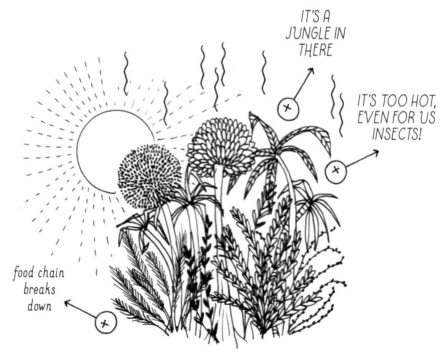

IT'S A JUNGLE IN THERE

IT'S TOO HOT, EVEN FOR US INSECTS!

food chain breaks down

tropical high temperatures

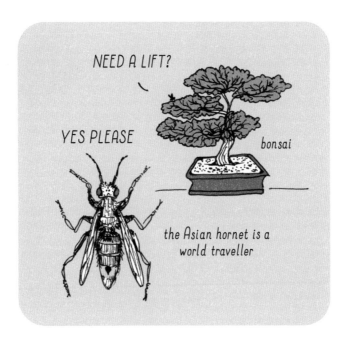

NEED A LIFT?

YES PLEASE

bonsai

the Asian hornet is a world traveller

84 THE WASP THAT LIKES BEES

Bees are having a really hard time (see Fact 29). There are far fewer than there used to be, if you'll pardon the pun! Their numbers just keep falling. That's partly due to a particular pesticide that is used to spray crops. Bees that swallow the poison often don't live though the winter. It is also difficult for honey bees to keep their queen alive. Without a queen the whole hive dies. Luckily, the European Union has now banned that poison.

Our honey bees are also under threat from the **Asian hornet**, a large wasp that's 2.5 to 3 centimetres long. European bees know the common wasps that have lived here for a long time. When the bees are attacked, they surround the wasp and kill it. But they don't recognize the Asian hornet. It can invade a beehive and steal everything. It probably arrived in France in 2004 with a load of bonsai trees from Asia. Five years later there were already thousands of Asian hornet nests all over the country. They can now be found in England, Italy, Belgium and the Netherlands. If you see an Asian hornet, you should report it to the authorities. It has black feet with bright yellow tips. Its face is orangey red. The segments on its back are yellowy orange. Asian hornet nests are destroyed. Although we like all insects, we don't when they kill our bees.

85 SWITCH OFF THE LIGHTS, PLEASE, AND GIVE US A BIT OF PRIVACY

is that the sun?

Maybe you haven't heard the term **light pollution** before and you find it a bit strange. How can light pollute? But it does. We're talking about artificial light that helps you see at night: street lights, high light masts along motorways, lights in football stadiums, the lighting outside various kinds of buildings and so on.

Of course it's a good thing for our streets to be lit at night, but it does confuse the insects. Nearly half of all insects are nocturnal. They need darkness to survive. Some don't mate if the lights are on. Artificial light changes the 'smell' signals that the females give off and they can no longer attract males. Without fertilization they cannot reproduce. Female **fireflies**, for instance, don't light up as much in artificial light, so it is harder for the males to find them. It's a lonely night for both of them.

Insects such as **dung beetles** need a starry sky to find their way. They have a special part of the body that can 'read' the position of the moon and stars. They need to do that to take balls of dung back to their nests. The artificial light confuses them completely.

Sometimes artificial light even disturbs the life of insects that are active during the day. **Bees** are diurnal, but they come out when there is a lighted area close to their nest. They have too little sleep and get exhausted. If they don't recover from their nocturnal journeys, they die. So just use a torch if you go out at night. That way you will give insects a bit of privacy.

OK, YOU WIN!

there's too much competing light for female fireflies

86 SOME LOSERS, SOME WINNERS, FOR THE TIME BEING

For most animals, climate change and environmental pollution are a problem. When the ice at the North Pole melts, **polar bears** have a difficult time. They are good swimmers, but there are no fish. It's much more difficult for them to hunt seals and other food in the water. Without sea ice they have nowhere to rest. It's almost impossible for them to find a mate. And even if they do, there is no snow left where they can make a den. Polar bears are already having trouble adapting to the changing conditions at the North Pole and in Greenland. If they don't manage to, they won't survive. So they are a seriously endangered species.

For other animals, the warmer oceans are not such a problem at the moment. For some whale species it is actually a good thing. With less ice it is easier for **whales** to swim to other places. So their feeding area gets wider and they have more chances to meet other whales and get together to have more young. But that will not last. When the ecosystem changes, the life of these whales changes too. Without coral there might not be enough krill and they won't have enough to eat. So there must be a balance. It might seem as if some animals are doing well due to climate change for the time being, but it is likely they will lose everything in the long run.

87 ARE THERE ANY SOUTH CHINA TIGERS LEFT?

Twenty years ago there were 10,000 **endangered plant and animal species** on the **red list** of the International Union for Conservation of Nature (IUCN). In 2019 there were **more than 30,000** – that's over three times as many.

So far scientists have identified 1.4 million plant and animal species, including mammals, birds, fish, insects and other reptiles, invertebrates, amphibians, plants and fungi.

More and more animals and plants are being added to the **IUCN** orange and red lists because their numbers are dangerously low. They are dying out as they lose their habitats due to environmental pollution and climate change or because they are being hunted by poachers. As many as 30,000 animal and plant species on the red list face extinction. That is 25% of all mammals, 14% of bird species, 30% of sharks and rays, 33% of coral, 34% of all coniferous trees and 41% of all amphibians.

Seriously endangered mammals include black rhinos, orangutans, Taiwanese white dolphins, gorillas and Wondiwoi tree kangaroos. There are only a few hundred left. But it gets worse. We know for certain that some species will become extinct in the next few years. Eighteen or so Californian porpoises are left. Poachers try to catch and sell them. Sometimes they get caught up in nets. Barely 60 Javanese rhinos have survived. They are poached because some people believe their horn has healing powers. Twenty Hainan gibbons are left on the Chinese island of Hainan. Their habitat is too small and it is hard for them to breed. The future also looks bleak for the 50 northern sportive lemurs on Madagascar. And we don't know if there is even a single South China tiger left.

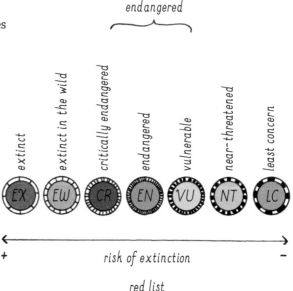

WOW!

European bee-eater
Merops apiaster

SLAP

Asian tiger mosquito
Aedes albopictus

as it gets warmer, more creatures are going on holiday in the north

88 BEE-EATERS ... BUT TIGER MOSQUITOES TOO

Have you heard of **bee-eaters?** They are magnificent birds with brightly coloured plumage. They usually breed in southern Europe, but as the summers get warmer they are starting to move further and further north. European bee-eaters have already been spotted in Belgium. Their distant cousin, the green bee-eater, which normally breeds in North Africa and Asia, has also been seen in northern Europe. They eat bumblebees, dragonflies, butterflies and honey bees. It is certainly unusual for these birds to be able to survive here. The only conclusion: it must have something to do with the warmer climate.

Unfortunately it's not just beautiful birds that come north now that it's warmer. Exotic **mosquitoes** are now being seen as far up as the Netherlands and Belgium. They are a threat because they can carry all kinds of viruses. For instance, the **Asian tiger mosquito** can bring in dengue, yellow fever or zika. They travel in passengers' luggage or with all kinds of imported goods. Mosquitoes used not to be able to survive in the northern climate, but they can now that it's getting warmer. Tiger mosquitoes are easy to recognize. They are very small, with black and white striped bodies and white stripes on their feet. Scientists are keeping an eye on them to make sure they can't cause any epidemics.

89 FAREWELL PLANTS

You might think that extinction is something that only happens in faraway lands. But it isn't just tropical areas where animals and plants are becoming endangered, or even extinct. Some species in Europe are disappearing too. Did you know that Belgium used to have more than 50 species of **orchids?** Now at least six species have already disappeared and the future is not looking

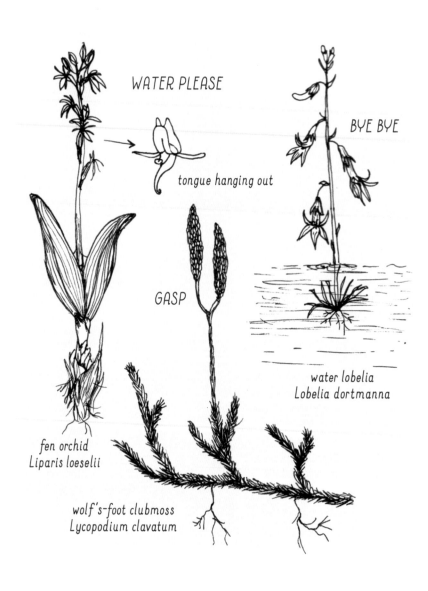

WATER PLEASE

tongue hanging out

BYE BYE

GASP

water lobelia
Lobelia dortmanna

fen orchid
Liparis loeselii

wolf's-foot clubmoss
Lycopodium clavatum

good for the others. The **fen orchid**, for example. It doesn't have big colourful flowers like those you see in flower shops; it is a less flashy plant with smaller flowers. It needs plenty of water to grow. Belgium is getting drier because of global warming and the fen orchid is not getting enough water. The plant is protected but it's not doing well. In 2017 and 2018 only a couple were found in the Flanders region.

The same goes for **wolf's-foot clubmoss**, a plant that has existed since the age of the dinosaurs. It has been through a lot in its long existence, but now it's getting rarer and rarer. It's very vulnerable to long dry periods like heatwaves. That's sad, because it is used in all kinds of medicines. For instance, it can help Alzheimer's sufferers with memory problems.

The **water lobelia**, the **European black poplar** and other plants are not doing well either. Global warming could finally push them over the edge.

90 WHAT IF ONLY FEMALES ARE BORN?

With humans and other mammals it's known immediately after fertilization whether their young will be male or female. But it's not the same for lizards, turtles and snakes or for crocodiles. For them, the sex of the offspring is determined by the temperature at which the egg is hatched. That is called **temperature-dependent sex determination**.

Smart people know straight away what that means. When the temperature changes, a lot of (or only) males or females are born. Take **sea turtles** for example. They bury their eggs on the beach. In high temperatures mostly females are born, at low temperatures mostly males. When the temperature goes up a couple of degrees too many, female turtles come out of the eggs. That can mean the destruction of the species. How are the females to be fertilized if there are no males left? Besides that, in warmer water the young are smaller and not so strong. With **crocodiles** it is exactly the opposite. At temperatures over 32°C, mostly males are born and at temperatures under 30°C mostly females. So you can see the huge impact that a couple of degrees' difference can have on an animal population.

DATE NIGHT

CLICK → ENTER

I'm not sure we'd be all that compatible!

climate refugees

91 MASS EXODUS

Sometimes, it becomes impossible to live in certain places and there is a mass exodus. People leave their homes and belongings to find shelter somewhere else. In the past that was often because of a war or because they were not safe in a particular country. Nowadays there are also **climate refugees**. People have to move because rising sea levels cause floods that sweep their houses away. Or the region where they live has now become a dry desert and there is not enough drinking water any more. Or nothing can grow because of drought and they have nothing to eat. They might also be fleeing a natural disaster like a hurricane, a tsunami or an earthquake. When people flee they often end up in places that have their own problems. That can lead to conflicts and even civil wars.

The first recognized climate refugees are people from the island of **Tuvalu** in the Pacific. Since 2014 they have been allowed to move to New Zealand because there's a good chance that in a few years their island will disappear completely into the sea. Asia and Africa are also seriously affected. The drought in the Gobi Desert has driven thousands of Chinese farmers into the nearby cities. Bangladesh is a densely populated country, a large part of which is barely above sea level. Hundreds of thousands of people have had to flee the rising water. Even in North America people are fleeing climate change. Inhabitants of Isle de Jean Charles, an island in Louisiana, have had to move because their island was constantly under water. And a lot of people from the states of New York and New Jersey were driven from their homes by a violent hurricane. In California it is the forest fires that drive people out.

Researchers estimate that the number of climate refugees will continue to rise every year. In 2050 it might be around 150 to 300 million people. Did you know that 300 million is more than the populations of Germany, France, Britain and Italy put together, all on the move?

92 THE POOR SOUTH IS PAYING THE HIGHEST PRICE

A person living in a poor country emits much less CO_2 than someone in a richer country. The amount of water an average person in parts of Africa uses in a day equals the same amount that we just flush down the toilet in one day. And yet the poor countries are the main victims of global warming. They are hit hardest by drought and floods. There are fewer and fewer fish in the sea and in large lakes in Africa, so people have less to eat. Also, people often can't afford to protect themselves better against various disasters.

Obviously, that's not fair. Really, it's the poor who are paying the price for all of us. So it's only fair that the rich industrial nations look for solutions to counter the effects of climate change in poorer countries in the south. That is called **climate justice**. We also need to make sure that fast developing countries like China and Brazil can grow without increasing their CO_2 emissions even more or further polluting the environment. That can only be done if we share our knowledge with all other countries and join together to look for solutions that make life better for everyone, without causing more harm.

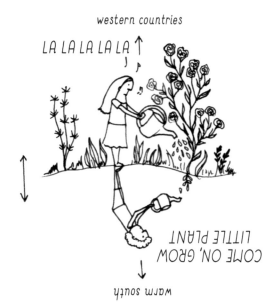

6

WHAT ARE WE GOING TO DO ABOUT IT?

clever clogs →

GOOD IDEA

COOL PLAN

BFF

PEACE AND LOVE

WHAT A TEAM

BUNCH OF HIPPIES

climate conference

93 IT CAN ONLY SUCCEED IF WE ALL WORK TOGETHER

Now that you've read all the information on the climate, you'll know that we are facing a huge **challenge**, perhaps the biggest challenge ever for the human race. Luckily, more and more of us are realizing that we are running out of time. Smart people are working hard to find solutions. They are looking for ways to produce things with fewer raw materials, less energy, fewer greenhouse gas emissions and less toxic materials. The effects of global warming and environmental pollution are now being felt in many places and they are trying to find ways for people and the environment to adapt to each other.

Climate conferences are attended by governments, scientists, business leaders and representatives from all kinds of organizations and are being held all over the world. They set **climate targets** based on scientific information collected by the IPCC (see Fact 41) and decide when the goals are to be achieved.

In 1997 an important document was drawn up in the Japanese city of Kyoto: the **Kyoto Protocol**. The industrial countries (apart from the United States) agreed to cut greenhouse gas emissions. By 2012 emissions were to be reduced by an average of 5% compared with 1990. Between 2013 and 2020 they were to be 18% lower than in 1990. A climate conference has been held every year since 2013. Under an important new international climate agreement signed in Paris by 195 countries in 2015, we have to try to limit global warming to 1.5°C compared with the average temperature between 1850 and 1900. The temperature must certainly not rise by more than 2°C if we are to preserve the quality of life for human beings. Every country has to draw up a climate plan and explain how it will reduce greenhouse gases. The rich countries have to help the developing countries bring down CO_2 emissions. The agreements are a first step. Now we have to wait and see how far they are put into practice. President Trump has already announced that the United States no longer wants to take part.

Sustainability basically means using the earth in such a way that our children, grandchildren, great-grandchildren and great-great-grandchildren can live here too. To do that we need to find a balance between people, the environment and the economy.

The **United Nations** has published a document setting out 17 sustainable goals that can be achieved by countries by 2030.

All of these goals are connected. They are to do with people, the environment, climate, prosperity and justice.

The first aim is to reduce all forms of **poverty**. In the last 20 years poverty has fallen worldwide but one in every 10 families still has to live on less than about £1.50 a day. At the same time we need to try to wipe out hunger from the world. There is enough food for everyone, as long as we grow it, share it out and consume it sustainably. Children all over the world have a right to a good education. Boys and girls must have the same opportunities. Adults have the right to a good reasonably paid job.

Of course, the goals are also to do with the **environment** and **climate**. We have to make sure we produce clean energy and reduce CO_2 emissions. Factories need to be less polluting. We need to use raw materials and available energy more carefully. Rich countries must help poor countries move to a clean and sustainable economy. We have to make sure that new trees are planted and no more forests are cut down anywhere in the world.

Those are fine goals, but they mean that countries have to work together much more than they have up to now. There's no doubt that is the biggest challenge.

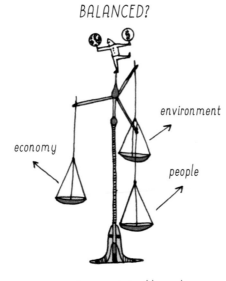

BALANCED?

economy

environment

people

seventeen sustainable goals

95 SQUID TO MAKE ECO-FRIENDLY PLASTIC

AHA!

... and a little squid protein

Can you picture it? A big laboratory with **squid** behind white tables, holding all sorts of test tubes in their tentacles. It's an entertaining picture but obviously that's not really how squid are helping us. They do have something that scientists are experimenting with. On their tentacles they have round suction cups with small teeth. The teeth help them grip their prey better. Some squid species have a special protein in their teeth (**squid ring teeth protein**, SRT), which can be used to make a kind of bioplastic. The plastic is very useful for adding a waterproof layer to raincoat or tent canvas material, for instance. It becomes

waterproof immediately. If the material tears, it can be 'grown' back together again. The plastic keeps its strength and can be washed without harmful plastic particles going into the water.

The best thing of all is that the plastic can be made without killing any squid. Scientists can make it themselves, using special bacteria. So the poor old squid doesn't have to lose its life to make the world a little better.

96 MEASURING IS KNOWING 1: CLIMATOLOGISTS PREDICT THE FUTURE

OOOOH! BOING tipping point

Scientists are always trying to predict the future. That's what they call **scenarios**. Scenarios are important, especially in climatology. They're based as little as possible on guesswork. Climatologists work on hard facts and figures. They want to measure and count what's happening. They want

to carry out experiments to find out if certain results are correct. Based on their measurements they try to understand how nature and climate work and what influence human beings have on them. The scenarios allow them to look into the future. For instance, they can predict what will happen if we just go on as we are. So 'no elephants left in 2050' and 'a 4°C rise in temperature' are not something seen in a crystal ball. They are scenarios that scientists are certain about.

We have already mentioned that climate change is fairly slow. But scientists are worried about **tipping points**. These are points at which something irreversible happens, something we can't go back on. We need to act before then.

A good example of a tipping point is the ice melting at the poles. Supposing all that ice is melting because of global warming: that is a tipping point because a fall in temperature will not be enough to get the ice back. Without ice at the poles, everything on earth will change. It is not certain if plants, people and animals will survive. Scientists are trying to predict how much more ice can melt and how warm it can get before we reach the tipping point. They are making **climate models** using data from the past and combining them with new measurements. The climate models help them find out how resilient the planet is. When can the system still be restored and when is that no longer possible?

The better scientists can predict tipping points, the better they can inform and advise us. It is then up to governments, to business and to us to do something before it's too late.

97 MEASURING IS KNOWING 2: ALGAE HELP CLIMATOLOGISTS

At the moment, scientists are forecasting that the temperature will rise by 1.5 to 4.5°C if the carbon dioxide in the atmosphere stays at its present level. That isn't really an accurate forecast. We now know that warming by 1°C makes an enormous difference. So the 3°C 'margin' between 1.5 and 4.5 is very important.

To be able to forecast accurately, scientists use material from the ocean bed. They collect **fossilized algae** millions of years old. Algae feed on carbon dioxide. Their favourite is the 'light' kind of CO_2. If that is available they will not eat the heavier CO_2. So scientists look at the type of CO_2 in the fossilized algae.

Sometimes they find algae that fed on the heavier type. At the time there was very little carbon dioxide in the water and the atmosphere. By combining that information with other data from the past they have a better idea what effect an increase or reduction in the carbon dioxide level has on climate. Scientists are also discovering that these days the climate is changing faster than ever before. Things that normally happen over millions of years now take scarcely one hundred. With all that information they are better able to predict how sensitive climate and temperature are to carbon dioxide. But what's truly amazing is that something as small as algae can help them do this.

algae are fussy eaters!

98 MEASURING IS KNOWING 3: FORECASTS WITH A PINCH OF SALT

If you've ever swallowed a mouthful of seawater then you'll know that it's really **salty**. But did you know that the saltier the seawater is, the heavier it is? Heavy water sinks, creating **currents** in the seas and oceans that strongly influence the climate. Climatologists want to find out how salty the water can become before currents change or stop flowing altogether.

The water at the North and South Poles is very salty. As saltier water is heavier, it sinks, creating a current. The relationship between the saltiness and temperature also plays a big role in creating currents. A lot of water evaporates around the equator because it is very warm. That raises the salt content of the seawater, certainly in places where there is little rainfall. Warm water is lighter than cold water, and so it carries on floating. When it flows to the poles it cools down and so sinks. Deep below the surface it flows back

to the equator again to replace the lowest layer of warm water flowing away.

But as we've learned, the climate is warming up. As the ice melts, more fresh and therefore 'lighter' water flows into the seas and oceans. That can slow down or even stop the force that drives the current. If climatologists understand better how salinity creates currents, they can predict a tipping point. They want to learn at what point is water not salty enough to keep the world's ocean currents moving?

To study the saltiness of the ocean, they look for tiny plankton, algae and shellfish fossils. They measure their saltiness or **salinity** inside and out. By combining the results with various types of information they are able to make predictions that you really shouldn't take with a pinch of salt.

YEP, SALTY!

plank-tongue

taste test

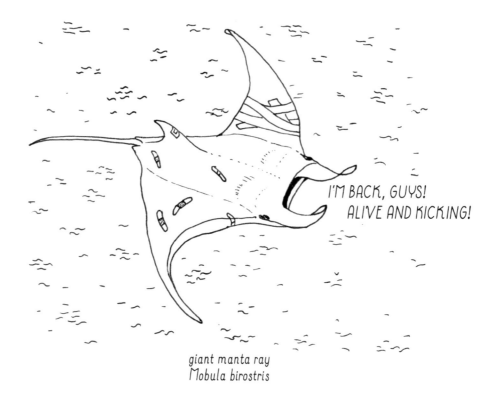

giant manta ray
Mobula birostris

99 NATURE CAN RECOVER IF YOU LET IT

Luckily, there are times when the natural world can be very resilient. Anything that is damaged can recover, provided that we give it a chance and stop making it even worse.

A good example is the **ocean** in the **Raja Ampat islands** in South-East Asia. Because of overfishing and mismanagement there were hardly any sharks or other large fish left. The reef was dying. Luckily, in 2007 the government decided to protect the waters around the islands. Ten years later they're full of **sharks!** Sharks even go there to give birth. The turtles that were once hunted graze peacefully on the seabed. With the arrival of the sharks, other large fish such as **giant manta rays** came back too. It is almost miraculous how quickly the ocean has recovered.

Another example is the **Atacama Desert** in South America. Once, millions of sea birds flocked there, but 50 years ago they disappeared. The area had been overfished and the birds no longer had enough to eat. The government decided to protect the coastal waters. Large shoals of **anchovies** came back. After a while the birds also returned. Now there are 3 million **cormorants** on the coast again. The pelicans came back too, and so did the sealions, which also like to eat anchovies.

Nature can recover quickly when we give it a chance. Scientists believe that if a third of all our coastal waters are restored to health, nature can recover enough to provide food for every human and animal.

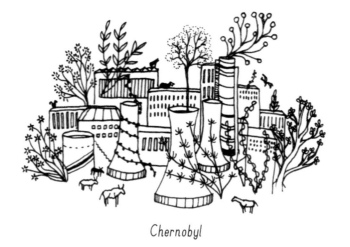

Chernobyl

100 NATURE TAKES OVER AGAIN WHEN THERE ARE NO PEOPLE AROUND

In 1986 there was a terrible disaster in Ukraine, a country in Eastern Europe. A **nuclear power station** reactor blew up in the town of **Chernobyl**. More than 100,000 people had to flee the radiation. The town had to be completely evacuated.

It will still be a long time before Chernobyl is safe for people. But something extraordinary is happening. The buildings, houses and streets are being taken over by greenery. Trees are growing through the roofs of the houses. All kinds of plants and trees are growing where a factory used to be. The asphalt on the roads is being pushed up by bushes.

Wild animals have also returned. At the moment Chernobyl is home to foxes, lizards, salamanders and many different birds. Scientists visiting the site also see a lot of large mammals such as deer, eland and brown bears. There is even a herd of Przewalski's horses, which were thought to be almost extinct in the wild. And there are a lot of wolves. They only come if there is enough prey for them to hunt. In thirty years, nature has managed to recover. The place where a town once stood has now gone back to nature. There is still **radiation** there, but that does not seem to have all that much effect on the animals. If people come back to live there there's no doubt the animals and nature will disappear again. Apparently human beings are more of a threat to nature than atomic radiation.

101 NATURE IS MORE PRODUCTIVE IF YOU LEAVE IT ALONE

In some parts of Africa, it's often very hard for farmers to grow their crops. They sometimes have to sow up to four times before anything grows. That's because there is not enough water in the soil and the wind cuts across the land like a knife, making it hard for plants to thrive.

Quite by accident, farmers in **Niger** in West Africa discovered that it was better to leave trees and bushes standing and not cut them down. They found that out by chance. Outside the farming season a lot of the young men worked in the city. When they returned the land was overgrown with **trees and bushes**. Some of them came back so late that they didn't have time to clear their fields. They planted the seeds on fields where trees and bushes were still growing.

To their surprise, the farmers who left the trees and bushes had better harvests than those who had cleared them. Exactly the same happened the following year. The farmers decided not to 'empty' their fields any more. They left the trees and bushes as they were. The trees sheltered the fields against the wind and shaded the crops growing there. The water in the ground did not evaporate as quickly and there was more left for the plants. The leaves that dropped from the trees fed the soil. The farmers have now learnt a lot more about forestry. The greening of over 5 million hectares of agricultural land in Niger only took a couple of years. That is an enormous amount of land. In fact, all the farmers did was let nature take its course. They did not plant trees specially; they just let the ones that were already there grow. It was both cheap and effective.

before

after

MUCH BETTER

102 THE BEAVER IS BACK!

Most people know what **beavers** look like. They are instantly recognizable with their big flat tail which they can slap on the ground to warn other beavers of danger. But a beaver's tail is also a useful tool for building a dam and it provides shade for their young. In the mid-19th century, beavers had been almost wiped out in Europe. They were hunted for their coats and meat. Beavers were only found in a few places in Norway, Russia, Poland and Germany. But at the end of the 20th century, they were spreading to a lot of European countries again. Their habitats were protected. They were able to build as many dams and lodges* there as they wanted. A beaver dam really is a small miracle of technology. It alters the whole landscape. Hundreds of hectares of marshland develop and attract other animals. The area in and around the beaver dam teems with life. By 2003 there were around 600,000 beavers in the whole of Europe. If you'd like to see one yourself, you can go with a guide to a nature reserve and spot beavers in the early evening.

BONUS FACT

As well as beavers, **otters** are also slowly returning. In the 1960s they almost became extinct in Britain because of water pollution. Luckily, otter numbers are now rising again.

* A lodge is the name given to a beaver's home. The entrance is usually under water.

103 WELCOME, MR WOLF!

Until the middle of the 19th century, **wolves** were living all over Europe. Perhaps it was fairy tales where the wolf was often the villain that made people afraid of them? Had wolves eaten their sheep once too often? Whatever the reason, all the wolves were killed. Wolf families, or **packs**, only survived in wild regions of Eastern Europe.

Since then a small miracle has occurred. Wolves are slowly but surely coming back, first and foremost because they have been protected in the European Union since 1982. They can no longer be hunted. When the border between Eastern and Western Europe opened up again at the end of the 20th century, the wolves were curious and came to have a look. As soon as they saw that there was enough food, they spread further afield. The wolves also became less shy of people. They were brave enough to come closer to places where people were living.

Wolves are at the top of the **food chain**. They mostly eat roe deer, red deer and wild boar. So they can make an ecosystem healthy again. The prey animals usually stay away from the area where the packs are. That allows the forest where the wolves live a chance to grow back, since the deer no longer nibble on the bark of the young trees. Wolves attract other animals, scavengers such as foxes, ravens, buzzards and badgers that feed on what the wolves leave behind. There are now more than 17,000 wolves in Europe, although none in the UK. Should we be afraid of them? Certainly not! Wolves stay out of your neighbourhood. And what about livestock? Yes, a tasty sheep is easy prey. But nature conservation organizations help farmers protect their sheep and other livestock against wolves. If a sheep is eaten, they get compensation from the government. So it's a good thing that wolves are coming back.

WHAT'S THE TIME, MR WOLF?

104 A LESSON ABOUT SNOW LEOPARDS

MOBILW

LOOK CHILDREN, THE SPIRIT OF THE MOUNTAINS!

Bayarjargal Agvaantseren

Once upon a time, thousands of **snow leopards** roamed through the Himalayas and then across the Chinese plateau. Not that they were seen all that often. Snow leopards are actually very shy creatures. That's why local people call them 'spirits of the mountains'.

Although they kept themselves well hidden, snow leopards had a hard time. Herders killed them because they sometimes attacked their livestock. Hunters shot them for their magnificent coats. Their habitat shrank as more and more roads and mines were built in those areas. The snow leopard became an endangered species. But then **Bayarjargal Agvaantseren** came along. Bayarjargal lived in a remote part of **Mongolia**. She was a teacher at a local school. Because she spoke several languages, she sometimes acted as a guide for foreign visitors. Then, one day she helped a foreign biologist who was doing research into the snow leopards. She fell completely under the animal's spell and quickly decided to do what

she could to prevent its extinction. She made sure herders had strong enclosures for their livestock. A special insurance scheme was introduced so that herders could claim compensation if one of their animals was killed by a snow leopard. The leopards' habitat needed to be widened, and for that the **mines** had to go. In 2009 Bayarjargal started campaigning for the government to close down the mines. That was the only way to enlarge the snow leopards' habitat. And she succeeded! Tost Tosonbumba Nature Reserve is an huge area covering over 700,000 hectares. The last mine was closed in June 2018.

In 2019 Bayarjargal was awarded the **Goldman Prize** for her work. That is a sort of green Nobel Prize for activists who make a special contribution to protecting the environment. It has been awarded to six people every year since 1990. Bayarjargal said she would use the money to continue fighting for the snow leopard.

105 WHAT IF PACKAGING WAS EDIBLE?

Packaging that's made from natural ingredients? What a great idea! Lots of work is being done in this field. For instance, it can be made of **beeswax**, which is completely biodegradable. You peel it off just like you'd peel a tangerine. You can pack some things in a caramelized sugar wrapping with a layer of wax on it. Then, you can

crack the packaging open like an egg. The sugar just dissolves in water and there's no waste. What about a package you can pour boiling water into? The food inside is cooked and at the same time the packaging turns into a bowl you can eat from. The bowl is completely biodegradable. Pretty cool, eh?

How about a milk-based food wrapper that you can eat? You put your packet of instant soup and the wrapper into a bowl and pour boiling water over it. The packet dissolves completely and you drink it along with your soup. It's hoped this **edible wrapper** will be able to replace all our plastic wrap in the future. It also protects food as much as five hundred times better than normal plastic wrap because it keeps out oxygen and food stays fresher. These are all things we can look forward to and they are also great ideas.

tasty bag
crunchy box (crisps)
filling packet (chips)
delicious package (biscuits)
crispy bottle (soft drinks)

YUM, AND THE BISCUITS TASTE GOOD TOO!

106 KEEPING CITIES COOL

As we saw in Fact 78, when the temperature rises, cities get really hot. That's because cities have a lot of dark surfaces that don't reflect the sun's rays. They are absorbed by the surface and radiate heat. Traffic and factories emit more heat. Cities are increasingly becoming **heat islands**, places where it is unhealthily hot for people and animals.

So smart urban planners, people who design cities and towns, are looking for ways to keep cities cool. Obviously, it's impossible to install a huge air conditioning system. Anyway, that would use too much energy. Luckily, there are other solutions.

The black **asphalt** on the streets, squares, car parks and roofs absorbs a lot of heat. By covering it with a **reflective layer** that reflects sunlight we can bring the temperature down in summer. We can also plant trees and bushes on the roofs of houses and buildings. **Green roof gardens** hold water and have a cooling effect. **Rainwater** can be collected in special tanks where the water evaporates as it warms up. Engineers are now looking for ways to make buildings retain or hold

water, for instance by using alternative building materials, not cement or concrete. Then the water can evaporate slowly and this would cool down the whole city. Clever idea, isn't it?

Fewer cars, more cycle paths and better public transport also help to keep the city cooler and more livable. In 50 years' time, most cities will certainly look very different.

smart city of the future

107 CLEAN THE AIR BY CYCLING

We all want to breathe clean air, right? But if you live in a big city that's sometimes easier said than done. Because of traffic, factories and other pollutants we inhale a lot of fine particles. **Daan Roosegaarde** has designed an enormous vacuum cleaner that breathes in dirty air and breathes out clean air. The **Smog Free Tower** is about 7 metres high and uses minimum energy, less than a kettle! The tower can clean about 30,000 square metres of air in a single hour, in a park for instance. It is 42% carbon, the material diamonds are made of. You can't make real diamonds out of it yet, but Daan Roosegaarde can get it crystallized. It's used to make rings and other jewellery. There are now Smog Free Towers in cities around the world, including Amsterdam and Beijing.

Daan Roosegaarde is even going a step further. He is working with a Chinese firm to make bicycles with a special device on their handlebars.

The **Smog Free Bicycle** filters the air in the same way as the tower. When there are lots of cyclists riding around the city, the air is automatically cleaned. Of course, you have to be prepared to cycle through the smog...

COUGH

clean air
OUT

CO_2
IN

The air is recycled, get it?

108 THE LIGHT SWITCHES ITSELF ON

People were probably thrilled when the **incandescent light bulb** was invented in the mid-19th century. After all it was a simple, clean and fast way of lighting your home. But light bulbs did not only give off light; in fact they also generated **heat**. The heat just got lost. So incandescent light bulbs were unlikely energy guzzlers. Now, they can no longer be sold in a lot of countries. They are being replaced by **energy-saving bulbs** or **LED bulbs**, which use as much as 80% less energy than the old-fashioned light bulbs.

Scientists are still searching for even more clean energy solutions. Now there are LED lamps with special sensors available. These react to what's happening around them. For instance, they can be fitted in street lights. When there isn't much movement, they give out less light or even no light at all. As soon as they sense movement, they shine brightly. This helps to reduce light pollution and energy consumption.

That's right, you are seeing red! In some places, red LED bulbs are being used for **street lights**. These are just as safe but they are often more animal-friendly. Red light doesn't disturb nocturnal animals quite as much. That's particularly good news for some slow-flying bats. With normal street lighting, they are easily preyed on by predators such as owls, but this is less of an issue when the lights are red. A street with red lights might seem a little bit unusual, but the bats are grateful for it!

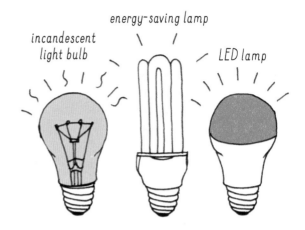

incandescent light bulb

energy-saving lamp

LED lamp

109 MUSSELS ARE A NATURAL FILTER

Mussels feed by filtering water. They mostly eat algae. Of course, there are other things in the water like rubbish, plastic and toxic substances.

Scientists are researching whether they can use certain species of mussels to filter water. For instance, **freshwater mussels** are used to remove blue-green algae from the water. These are

bacteria that contain a poison that's dangerous to people and other animals. The mussels eat them and this in turn keeps the water clear and clean.

Zebra mussels might be able to filter even more nasties out of the water. Tests are being carried out to see if mussels can remove microplastics from the water. Scientists are trying to find out if they can use shellfish to clean sewage. Instead of filters that need energy, mussels can do the work for nothing!

On the other hand, it's not so nice for the mussels. They are slowly but surely poisoned and in the end they die. So it's still a lot better not to dump so many toxic substances and waste in the environment. Then the poor mussels don't have to pay with their lives.

microplastic fragments

MUSSEL SORTING CENTRE

clean water

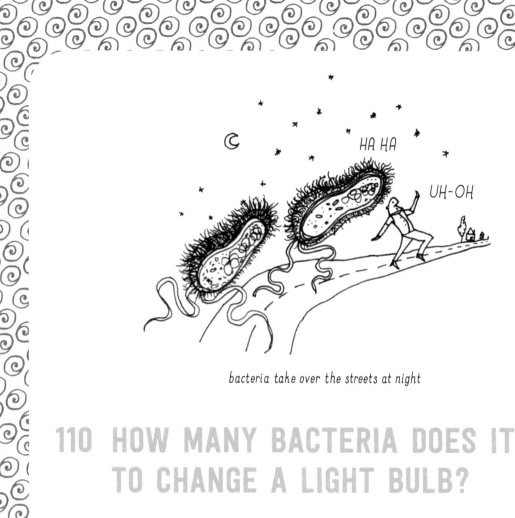

HA HA

UH-OH

bacteria take over the streets at night

110 HOW MANY BACTERIA DOES IT TAKE TO CHANGE A LIGHT BULB?

No, that isn't a joke. **Bacteria** really can create light. A young French scientist called **Sandra Rey** has been researching this for many years. When she was a child she saw a report about luminous jellyfish. The subject always fascinated her. As soon as she graduated she started experimenting. She wanted to identify the substances that cause **bioluminescence** in animals, making jellyfish and other fish and even some land animals light up in the dark. She extracted these substances from their genetic material (or DNA) and put them into the DNA of harmless bacteria. She put the bacteria in a large bowl of water and gave them sugar to eat. The bacteria multiplied very fast. The next day, the whole bowl was empty.

That's a very simple explanation and of course the way it works is a bit more complicated. But Sandra Rey believes that one day some of our light can be replaced by luminous bacteria. They give out a pale green light that doesn't disturb nocturnal creatures. And they can take any form. Her discovery is not yet perfect. Bacteria quickly die if they don't get any food and the light is still not strong enough. But it's a promising discovery. It will be interesting to see if one day, bacteria take over our streets!

111 CYCLING THROUGH THE STARRY NIGHT

You've probably heard of Vincent van Gogh, the famous Dutch painter. In 2015, all kinds of events were organized to commemorate him 125 years after his death. The artist Daan Roosegaarde came up with a fantastic way of paying tribute to Van Gogh and at the same time showing off a new kind of street lighting. It was to be a combination of art and new energy-saving technology. He covered a 600-metre cycle path with **luminous stones**. The pattern was based on Van Gogh's famous *Starry Night* painting. As you cycle along the path at night, you feel as if you're riding through a wonderful starry sky.

The stones in the path are charged by the sun during the day, then at night they give off light again. This is a very energy-saving, safe and beautiful alternative to normal street lighting. Now there are a lot of these **light-emitting cycle paths** in the Netherlands. They are really useful, especially in places where there are either very few street lights or none at all.

The system is now used on motorways too. Lines are drawn with a special coating (a sort of paint) that charges in the daytime and lights up at night. And because Daan Roosegaarde is an artist, they all look beautiful as well.

BONUS FACT

Daan Roosegaarde says it is especially hard to persuade politicians and business leaders to accept an idea. Often they say, 'yes, but' and look for all kinds of arguments against it. So he designed a special 'yes, but' chair. When you sit on it and say 'yes, but' you get a slight electric shock in your bottom. You're going to think twice before saying 'yes, but' ever again.

HOME!

starry night

112 NUCLEAR ENERGY DOESN'T CREATE GREENHOUSE GASES (BUT IT DOES CAUSE OTHER PROBLEMS)

Everything around us is made of tiny **atoms**. These are held together by a nucleus. When you split the nucleus it releases **nuclear energy**. We use uranium and plutonium to make nuclear energy. Uranium rods are put into a big steel vat with water. Then, they are bombarded with neutrons, splitting the uranium atoms. That causes a chain reaction and the nuclei split and release a lot of energy, heating the water in a large boiler. The steam drives a turbine that generates energy to supply the electricity network. In itself, nuclear energy is a very clean energy. No fossil fuels are used, so no greenhouse gases are emitted. Also, nuclear power stations can generate constant energy and they are usually very reliable.

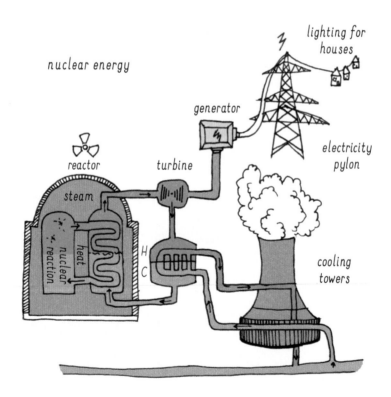

nuclear energy

lighting for houses

generator

electricity pylon

reactor

turbine

steam

nuclear reaction

heat

H
C

cooling towers

But unfortunately there are a couple of serious problems with nuclear energy. The waste produced in nuclear fission is **radioactive** and stays that way for ten thousand years! It has to be stored safely. That isn't easy. If there is a disaster like the tsunami that hit Fukushima, Japan, in 2011, a nuclear power station can be damaged and radioactivity is released into the environment. That is catastrophic for the people living nearby and even those further away. They are contaminated and can get very ill and even die. Nuclear power stations are also very difficult to build and it takes a long time. And besides that, quite a lot of CO_2 is emitted when mining uranium and building new nuclear power stations. Nuclear energy has its supporters and its opponents. So before building a new power station, it needs to be carefully considered whether there are in fact other ways to generate electricity.

113 DANCE AND MAKE YOUR OWN ENERGY

It looks as if Dutch university students in Eindhoven and Delft love to dance. They've designed a **dance floor** where you can actually generate real energy just by dancing! **Dynamos** beneath the dance floor pick up the impacts of all the dance steps and convert them into electricity. An evening's dancing can generate a third of all the electricity needed for a party. The faster you dance, the more **electricity** you make!

Of course, these floors can't only be used as dance floors. How about laying one in a school playground to generate electricity at playtime, which can then light the classrooms? Or in the stands of a football stadium? Thousands of supporters jumping up and down are certainly enough to keep the big lights on. Or a footpath or cycle path that lights up when you walk or cycle on it? Put your dancing shoes on!

SHAKE IT BABY

HOP

OOH YEAH!

on the floor

underneath the floor

charged battery

dancing for the climate

hot ball of energy

WHOOPS! NEARLY!

solar energy

114 THE SUN'S A BIG BALL OF ENERGY

The **sun** is a glowing ball with a surface temperature of as much as 6,000°C. That is scarcely imaginable. Inside it's even hotter, a staggering 15,000,000(!)°C. If a piece of iron got too close to the sun it would melt immediately. The sun is actually an enormous nuclear reactor. Energy is released and radiated as **light and heat**. It's enough to light and heat the earth, even though the sun is actually 149,598,000 kilometres away from us.

In one hour, the sun sends as much energy to the earth as the whole population consumes in a year. So it's no wonder that scientists try to capture that energy somehow. It can be done in various ways.

Solar panels convert sunlight into electricity. They are made of solar cells, two layers of silicon, a substance extracted from sand. When light shines on a **solar cell** an electric current is generated between the layers. About a fifth of the sunlight that is captured is then turned into electricity.

Solar collectors convert sunlight into heat. Water is heated by the sun in metal pipes or plates. It can be used for showers or baths or to heat rooms.

Solar energy is clean energy that can be used anywhere. Unfortunately, sometimes there's too little sunshine and other times there's too much. The surplus can be stored in batteries, but not every house is equipped for that at the moment. Did you know that we can do a lot more with solar energy? Scientists have calculated that if we installed solar panels on 1% of the Sahara Desert we would have enough electricity for the whole world.

115 WINDMILLS ARE AN ANCIENT FORM OF GREEN ENERGY

Years ago, someone realized that the wind can generate quite a lot of energy. Maybe he or she went out in a violent storm and got blown over! Then, a clever person worked out that you could use that to your advantage and built a **windmill** with wind-powered sails. That moved a millstone that could grind corn into flour.

IT WORKS!

the windmill man

The **wind turbines** you see today don't look like the old windmills, and they generate electricity instead of grinding corn. The wind powers the turbine sails. The energy goes to a generator and is turned into electricity, which is carried to a power station through thick cables. From there, it's distributed to homes and businesses. Often, the turbines are grouped together in what is called a **wind farm**. These days they are often positioned out at sea.

Wind power doesn't emit any greenhouse gases and the turbines can be built very quickly. But, sadly they do have a couple of disadvantages. Sometimes there is no wind, so they are not 100% reliable. Besides that, they are not always animal friendly. They cause problems for bats and birds as well as insects. In Germany 1.2 tons of insects are killed by wind turbines every year. That's equivalent to 2.4 billion moths. They are quite noisy and they can cast a long shadow on places where you don't want one. Also, some people aren't keen on having them in their backyards.

One modern wind turbine can supply about 2,000 families with electricity. When we work out how to store it properly, **wind energy** is definitely a sustainable energy source for the future.

AGAIN!

GO ROUND?

WHOOSH

YIPPEE!

bird-friendly wind turbine?

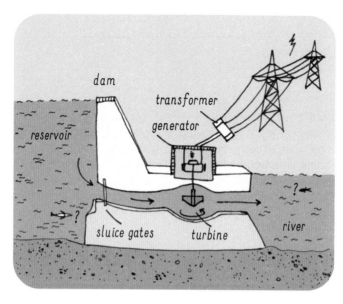

hydropower

116 THERE'S POWER IN WATER

If you've ever seen a waterfall, a really big one, you'll know how much power there is in falling water. So, a waterfall generates a lot of energy which we can use. The faster the water flows, the more electricity you can get from it. Countries with a lot of mountains and water can build **hydropower plants**. Norway, for instance, gets 98% of all its energy from hydropower.

To build a hydropower plant you need a dam. This holds the water back and a **reservoir** is formed. The water flows fast out of openings in the dam and turbines turn its power into electricity. So hydropower is clean energy and no greenhouse gases are emitted. The energy stored in the reservoir can be used at any time. But dams also have disadvantages. Life becomes more difficult for fish and other water creatures.

Dams and reservoirs disrupt whole ecosystems. And sometimes a lot of people have to move for dams and reservoirs to be built. When the **Three Gorges Dam** was built in China, over a million people had to look for somewhere else to live. In countries like the Netherlands and Belgium where the landscape is flatter, hydropower is a less important source of energy. Even so, both those countries have hydropower plants.

Now people are looking at ways of generating energy from the sea. The energy from tides and waves can be harnessed, as well as differences in salinity and temperature.

117 HEAT FROM INSIDE THE EARTH

Every day, the sun warms the earth. A lot of that heat is stored in the ground itself and in the ground water. That is called **ground source heat.** We can use it, for instance, to help heat buildings. The heat is brought up from the ground to a depth of 100 metres with a heat pump. That can be done for a house or for a whole neighbourhood.

It is boiling hot in the centre of the earth, as much as 6,000°C. We can use that heat too. It is called **geothermal energy**. You have to go down at least 500 metres to reach geothermal heat. In Iceland, it is used to heat most houses and buildings because Iceland is a volcanic island where the earth's heat is closer to the surface. The warm water is pumped up and the cooled water goes back down again.

Geothermal heat and ground source heat are clean energy sources with no greenhouse gas emissions. Unfortunately, it does cost a lot to set up heating networks that use them.

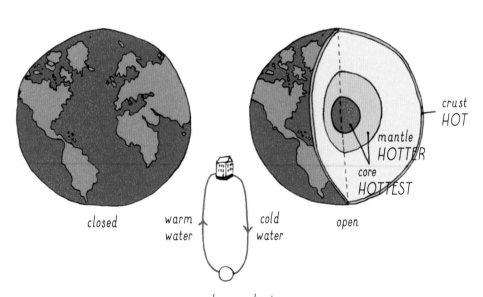

closed

warm water

cold water

crust
HOT

mantle
HOTTER

core
HOTTEST

open

ground source heat
geothermal energy

118 A CAR THAT RUNS ON SUGAR CANE

You've probably seen electric cars. To charge them, you just plug them into a power point. After a while, you can drive away. **Electric cars** don't emit greenhouse gases while you're driving them. Of course, car factories do emit CO_2 when they are manufactured. You also have to make sure the energy you're charging them with is from clean and sustainable sources.

Electric cars are getting better all the time, but now people are looking at other solutions, such as cars that run on hydrogen. Only water vapour comes out of the car exhaust, but you do need energy to make hydrogen. So you need to make sure it's sustainable. Also, you need a big tank and the right filling stations to be able to fill up with hydrogen and that's not so easy.

What about using plants as fuel? It's possible! In Brazil they make fuel from **sugar cane**. They crush the stalks, then let the juice ferment. This makes ethanol. Cars can run on it, but unfortunately it also emits CO_2. Planting new sugar cane takes carbon dioxide out of the air. Sadly, it's not a magic solution. Sugar cane plantations take up a lot of land, destroying the rainforest. So it's not a good idea for everyone to use sugar cane as fuel.

CARS OF THE FUTURE

plug-in

hydrogen

sugar cane

YES!
THE SUN'S OUT

Lightyear One
faster than the speed of light

119 SOLAR ENERGY RACE

The first World Solar Challenge was held in Australia in 1987. It's a **solar car** race across more than 3,000 kilometres of desert. It is organized to promote research into solar energy for cars and make it better known to the public.

Solar cars I hear you ask? Yes, there are cars that run on solar energy. They look pretty cool (or should we say 'hot'). They are made of very light materials and are really streamlined so there isn't too much air resistance. The engine is very economical and a lot of energy can be stored in the battery.

Would you like to own a solar car? The **Lightyear One** will be on sale in a couple of years. It is self-charging from sunlight, so it doesn't need any fuel or electricity. The solar cells are in the roof. The first solar cars will cost over £100,000. But you get a lot for your money! Not only can you actually drive around in the Lightyear One, you can also charge the other appliances in your house with it. What a fantastic invention!

120 DRASTIC ACTION

reflector time!

Climate experts know that global warming needs to be tackled without delay. We especially need to cut back our use of fossil fuels, oil and gas. Besides that, we need reforestation and clean oceans, so that more carbon dioxide is absorbed. But what if all that action doesn't have the results we were hoping for? Or if it takes too long? Scientists are thinking about that too. At that point they plan to take drastic action. They are talking about **climate engineering** or **geoengineering**, which uses all kinds of technology to alter the natural system, holding back the heat of the sun and storing CO_2. That might include **space shields** to block sunlight, **mirrors** in the desert that reflect sunlight back, ways of making large clouds that reflect sunlight, or **fertilizing** the oceans to grow more plankton which can absorb CO_2. They are also looking for ways to store carbon dioxide, for instance in salt mines or deep in the ocean, before it gets into the atmosphere.

The difficulty with all those **technologies** is that they can seriously affect the environment and the earth's various ecosystems. They might even make some problems worse instead of solving them. We all hope they won't be necessary.

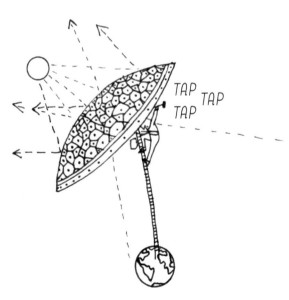

hammering on a space shield

121 WHAT YOU CAN DO

Most people are worried about the environment and the climate but they don't really want to make too many changes because they think it's too much effort. They say that what they're doing is just a drop in the ocean, meaning that the actions of one person make very little difference. But that's not true. A lot of drops can have quite a big impact. So here are a few tips for green living. You can start following them straight away.

THERE YOU GO

- Throw away as little rubbish as you can. Never drop paper, plastic or other rubbish on the street. Always put it in a **bin**. The awful plastic soup in our seas and oceans comes from litter.

WHICH ONE?

- **Sort rubbish** as much as you can, at home and outside. Glass, paper, plastic, green waste and so on are often collected and processed separately.

AAH

- Always drink **tapwater**. The water that comes out of our taps is just as healthy as bottled water

and it tastes as good. Plus it's as much as 300 to 400 times cheaper. Why would you ever buy another water bottle?

- Take your lunch to school in a **lunchbox**. Your sandwiches will taste twice as good. Of course you should already have a reusable drinks bottle.

YUMMY

- You don't need to **shower** every single day. It certainly isn't necessary in the winter. And besides that, it's better for your skin if it doesn't get wet every day.

_LA LA LA_

- Try not to stay in the shower for more than five minutes. How about asking your parents if you can use the kitchen timer? Rinse the shampoo out of your hair in good time so that you're ready when the bell rings! (Extra tip from us: You can even have a pee in the shower. That saves one flush of the toilet. Every little helps!)

- Turn the **tap** off while you're brushing your teeth. If you want, you can clean your teeth under the shower.

CLEAN!

dry brushing

122 WHAT ELSE CAN YOU DO?

- Do you have a smartphone? A laptop? A tablet? **Unplug** it as soon as it's charged. Otherwise you're wasting energy. And there's less wear on the battery.

- Switch off the **light** if you're the last person to leave the room. Switch off the TV, computer, laptop or tablet when you're not using them.

- When you're drawing or writing, use both sides of the **paper**. You can even reuse empty envelopes, printed paper and so on. And try to print out as little as possible.

- Don't use too much **toilet paper**. People who fold the sheets neatly before wiping usually use less paper than those who scrunch them up.

- Don't buy **so much stuff**. New clothes, new toys, – do you really need them all? Maybe you could ask to do something special on your birthday or at Christmas instead of getting presents.

- Try a **second-hand** or recycling shop for clothes and other things. You'll find a lot more there than you think! You can pimp up second-hand clothes or paint a second-hand cupboard yourself.

- Have you heard of **repair cafes?** They're places where you can have broken things fixed by experts. They also teach you how to repair things yourself. That's an added bonus if something else breaks down in the future.

123 WHAT YOU AND YOUR FAMILY CAN DO

We realize that your parents probably make a lot of decisions for you. Some things are a bit more difficult to change. But your family might be willing to do a few things with you.

- **Walk** or go by **bike** if you can. Maybe you can't walk or cycle to school every day, but you might manage it once a week. Or you could form a cycling group with kids in your area. You just need one adult to take it in turns each time. Public transport mostly emits CO_2, but you are sharing it with a lot of other people. Ask your parents to take you places or collect you by car as little as possible.

PEDAL!

- Do you eat meat every day? How about persuading your parents to go **vegetarian** once a week? Look for veggie recipes in the library or online. Your parents are going to be really pleased that you suddenly like vegetables!

CAULIFLOWER AGAIN?

- Ask if the **heating** at home could be turned down a bit. Soon you won't feel it, especially if you put on an extra sweater. And in the evening everyone can snuggle under a blanket.

HOT

- Use **single-use plastics** as little as possible: this means any kind of plastic that you throw away straight after you open something. It includes plastic water and soft drink bottles as well as all kinds of prepacked items in the supermarket. Do you go to the supermarket with your parents? If so, ask them to buy loose apples instead of the prepacked ones and put them in a reusable cloth or paper bag. You don't need separate bags for peppers, courgettes, aubergines and lots of other vegetables. They can be put in together.

TADAA!

BONUS TIP
Read out a fact from this book to your parents once in a while. It works!

Mathilda Masters is an explorer. She has made it her job to discover new continents and countries, which is not easy because most countries have already been discovered. Mathilda knows all there is to know about nearly every subject: animals, plants, history, science, language and a whole lot more.

Louize Perdieus studied graphic design and illustration at the Academy of Fine Arts in Antwerp. As a freelance illustrator she works on children's books and commissions for drawings. Her illustrations are full of humour and they appeal to people of all ages.

We found the information in this book in various places: books, national and international newspapers and magazines, documentaries and the websites of various organizations working on climate and the environment.

Books:
Sara L. Latta. *All About Earth: Discover Earth Science*. Raintree, 2015.

Vaclav Smil. *Harvesting the Biosphere*. MIT Press Ltd, 2015.

If you can, watch David Attenborough's fantastic *Our Planet* series. Other documentaries that are worth watching are Leonardo DiCaprio's *Before the Flood* (2016) and *A Plastic Ocean* by the journalist Craig Leeson (2016).

The websites of various organizations are a great source of information. Recommended sites are climatekids.nasa.gov, plasticsoupfoundation.org, greenpeace.org.uk, wwf.org.uk, European Environment Agency (eea.europa.eu).

Translated from the Dutch *123 superslimme dingen die je moet weten over het klimaat* by Lorna Dale

First published in the United Kingdom in 2020 by Thames & Hudson Ltd, 181A High Holborn, London WC1V 7QX

Original edition © 2019, Uitgeverij Lannoo nv, Tielt www.lannoo.com

This edition © 2020 Thames & Hudson Ltd, London

This book was published with the support of Flanders Literature (flandersliterature.be).

FLANDERS LITERATURE

British Library Cataloguing-in-Publication Data

A catalogue record for this book is available from the British Library

ISBN 978-0-500-29603-5

Printed and bound in Italy

To find out about all our publications, please visit **www.thamesandhudson.com**. There you can subscribe to our e-newsletter, browse or download our current catalogue, and buy any titles that are in print.